FONTIS
Published by
Fontis Publishing, Inc.
Canada

© 2007 Gerald de la Salle

All Rights Reserved

ISBN 978-0-9781285-4-8

Without limiting the rights under copyright reserved above, no
part of this publication may be reproduced, stored in or introduced
into a retrieval system, or transmitted, in any form, or by any means
(electronic, mechanical, photocopying, recording, or otherwise),
without the prior written permission of the copyright owner of this book.

Acknowledgements:
Cover Image by Laszlo-Photo
Translations: Park Hyeon-ju Ph.D., Keimyung University
Designer: James McKenzie

Visit us on the Web at:
GeraldDeLaSalle.com

Gerald de la Salle

Speaking! Speaking! Speaking!

English For Korean Beginners

Gerald de la Salle B.A., B.Ed., LL.B., M.A.
©2007

Visit us on the Web at:
GeraldDeLaSalle.com

Contents

	Contents
Unit 1: Conversational Basics	**13**
Dialogue	14
Dialogue	15
Basic Interview	16
Pronunciation	17
Numbers	18
Unit 2: Talking About You and Others	**19**
Dialogue	20
Interview	21
Verb: BE	22
Famous People	23
Interview	24
Questions	25
More Famous People	26
Numbers	27
Pronunciation	28
Unit 3: Do, Doing, and Other Verbs	**29**
Dialogue	30
Do/Does	31
Don't/Doesn't	33
Interview	34
Play	35
Interview	36
Interview	37
Accent Reduction	38
Pronunciation	39
Unit 4: Do, Doing, and Other Verbs 2	**40**
Dialogue	41
Interview	42
Schedule	43
Doing	44
Writing Questions	45
Accent Reduction	46
Game	47
Unit 5: More Verbs	**48**
Dialogue	49
Present Verbs	50
Collocations	51
Interview	52
Pronunciation	53
Unit 6: Have	**54**
Dialogue	55
Have	56
Interview	57
Grammar	58
Interview	59
How Many?	60
Interview	62

Contents

Pronunciation	63
Countries	64
Unit 7: Hobbies, Likes and Dislikes	**65**
Dialogue	66
Collocations	67
Hobbies	68
Interview	69
Hobbies	70
Dialogue	71
What Do You Think Of ...?	72
Interview	73
Dialogue	74
Nationalities	75
Pronunciation	76
Unit 8: Let's Go Out	**77**
Expressions	78
Dialogue	79
Let's Go To The Park	80
Let's	81
Conversation	83
Let's Go Out	84
Pronunciation	85
Unit 9: What Can You Do?	**86**
Dialogue	87
Interview	88
Dialogue	89
What Can She Do?	90
Pronunciation	91
Crossword	92
Dates	93
Unit 10: Your Routine	**94**
Dialogue	95
Words of Frequency	96
Interview	97
Interview	98
Specific Frequency	99
Interview	100
Pardeep's Schedule	101
Unit 11: Past Tense	**102**
Pronunciation	103
Dialogue	104
Y Verbs	105
Irregular Verbs	106
Past Tense	107
Past Tense	108
Interview	109
Game	111
Pronunciation	113

Contents

Unit 12: Past Tense (Part 2) — **114**
   Was/Were — 115
   Wasn't/Weren't — 116
   Interview — 117
   What Did You Do? — 118
   Schedule — 119
   Michael Jordan — 120
   Game — 121
   Pronunciation — 122

Unit 13: Future and Weather — **123**
   Dialogue — 124
   How's The Weather? — 125
   Will You...? — 126
   Will — 127
   Probability — 129
   Interview — 130
   Pronunciation — 131

Unit 14: Future and Weather (Part 2) — **132**
   Dialogue — 133
   Mun-hee's Vacation — 134
   Forecasts — 135
   Weather Forecast — 136
   Game — 137

Addendum: Verb-Noun Collocations — **139**
   Verb-Noun Collocations — 140

Addendum: Answers — **141**

Index — **142**

Introduction

I wrote this textbook 1) to assist beginners who are serious about learning to speak English; 2) to motivate large classes of Korean high school, college and university students to speak English during class time; 3) to clearly explain the English language in a user-friendly way so that beginners can learn English on their own; and 4) to provide English teachers with classroom materials that make it much easier to teach English Conversation. The main theme of the book is "Speaking! Speaking! Speaking!" It is designed to be used both in the classroom and for self-study.

Many English conversation teachers and professors in South Korea provide their students with little or no opportunity to speak English. This makes it difficult for students to improve their speaking ability. One reason why professors fail to provide students with ample opportunity to speak English is because their textbooks are seriously lacking conversational materials. Amazingly, some widely used English conversation textbooks in South Korea contain very few conversational activities. They typically have too many reading, writing and listening exercises and not enough speaking exercises. Further, many conversational textbooks fail to clearly explain the English language or provide user-friendly conversation activities. This lack of quality discourages students from speaking English and in turn causes teachers to try to "lecture" the language to their students or teach something other than "conversation." Without a proper conversation textbook, Korean students usually spend most of their class time speaking Korean or not speaking at all. Meanwhile, those who have a strong desire to learn English often complain that they don't get enough opportunity to speak English during their classes.

For these reasons, this textbook attempts to avoid the pitfalls of other English conversation books by providing a sufficient number and quality of speaking exercises. In my opinion, English conversation classes should be student-centered, where students spend much, if not most of their time, speaking English, usually chatting and speaking to one another in small groups of three to four people. In order to make this possible, students need an easy, straight forward, user-friendly textbook that provides appropriate speaking exercises to encourage them to speak English. It's my hope that the exercises in this textbook are so straight forward that students will have no difficulty understanding how to do them and that teachers won't need a teacher's manual. Just to be on the safe side, most of the instructions in the first few units are translated into Korean. Furthermore, almost every new

Introduction

word is translated so that students won't have to waste valuable classs time searching for words in their dictionaries or asking one another for translations. The textbook can be used in both small conversation classes or in large classes with fifty or more students.

Moreover, the textbook contains numerous examples, sample answers and translations so teachers don't have to waste valuable classroom time writing on the chalkboard, whiteboard, overhead etc. Many of the speaking exercises are lengthy with many questions. That is not an accident. It's my belief that learning to speak English requires extensive practice speaking the language. More questions mean more practice. Also, most of the example answers in the book illustrate A+ answers, rather than mere one-word responses or short utterances. For the purposes of this textbook, an A+ answer usually contains a fully, independent statement, which can be understood on its own, without any context. To significantly improve English speaking ability, students should try to answer questions without reading them. In other words, they should listen as their classmate(s) ask them questions. As well, it's more beneficial when students give A+ answers, rather than short responses.

In short, this textbook is designed to encourage students to keep speaking English and thereby improve their speaking ability. Reading and writing work is minimal. Most of the activities are conversational in nature and can be done in groups or with a partner. If you're a teacher, don't lecture. Let the students Speak! Speak! Speak!

Gerald de la Salle

Unit 1: Conversational Basics

• **VOCABULARY**: Study these words and then practice saying them with your class.

Address (*a-driss*) 주소
@ (at)
Because 왜냐하면
Blood type 혈액형
Business Card (*biz-niss-card*) 명함
Capital City (*ka-bih-doe-si-D*) 수도
Delicious (*D-li-shiss*) 맛있는
Engineer (*in-jin-eer*) 기술자
Excellent 훌륭한
Family name 성
Favorite 가장 좋아하는
First name 이름
Foreign (*For-rin*) 외국의
Given name 이름
Have coffee 커피 마시다
History (*His-tree*) 역사
Hometown 고향
Hospital (*Haws-bih-doe*) 병원
Last name (*Lass-naim*) 성
Lazy (*Lay-zee*) 게으른
Major (*May-jer*) 전공
Marketing 마케팅
Married 결혼한
Meeting (*Mee-ding*) 모임
President 대통령
Outside 바깥
Quebec 캐나다 동부의 주 이름
Sick 아픈
Single 미혼
Spell 철자를 말하다.
"Stay in touch" 연락하고 지내다
"Surfing the Internet" 인터넷을 하다
Textbook 교과서
Tall 키가 큰
Uncle 삼촌
(Underscore) ~에 밑줄을 긋다
"Work for" 근무하다

Dialogue

BASIC DIALOGUE 1. With your class and in groups, practice this conversation. Please refer to this dialogue when you do future exercises in this unit.
다음 대화를 연습하고, unit 1에 있는 연습문제를 공부할 때 참고 하세요.

A. How are you?
    B. *I'm fine. Thank you*.
A. My name is Kim Eun-ju. What's your name?
    B. *I'm* Larry Watson.
A. Nice to meet you Larry.
    B. *Nice to meet you too*.
A. Where are you from?
    B. *I'm from* Vancouver. How about you? Where are you from?
A. I'm from Pusan.
    B. Are you Korean?
A. Yes, I am. Where do you live?
    B. *I live in* Seoul. And you?
A. I live in Suwon.

BASIC DIALOGUE 2. Again, with your class and in groups, practice this conversation. 다시한번 다음 대화를 연습 하세요.

A. Hey Larry, what do you do?
    B. *I'm a sales person*. I work for a foreign company.
A. Where do you work?
    B. *I work in Seoul*.
A. Are you married?
    B. *Yes, I'm married*. Are you?
A. No, I'm single. How old are you?
    B. *I'm 30 years old*. How about you?
A. I'm 30 years old too. When is your birthday?
    B. My birthday is *August 3*.

Dialogue

Exercise 3

MATCHING. Please match the questions in Column A with the correct answers in Column B. 질문과 대답을 알맞게 연결 하세요.

QUESTIONS	ANSWERS
1. How are you? ____	A. I'm 21 years old.
2. What do you do? ____	B. Yes, I am.
3. Are you married? ____	C. I'm fine. Thank you.
4. Where do you live? ____	D. No. I'm single.
5. When is your birthday? ____	E. I'm from Quebec.
6. What is your email address? ____	F. I'm a student.
7. How old are you? ____	G. It's September 21.
8. What is your name? ____	H. I live in Daegu.
9. Where are you from? ____	I. It's type B.
10. What's your blood type? ____	J. It's single_korean_girl@hanmail.net
11. What's your major? ____	K. My major is marketing.
12. Are you French? ____	L. My name is Lee Hyun-ju.

Exercise 4

BASIC DIALOGUE 3. Again, with your class and in groups, practice this conversation. 다시한번 다음 대화를 연습 하세요.

A. Hey Larry! It was nice meeting you.
    B. Nice to meet you too.
A. Let's stay in touch.
    B. Okay. Maybe we can have coffee sometime.
A. Great! Do you have a business card?
    B. Sorry, not right now.
A. Well then, how do you spell your last name?
    B. *My last name is* W-A-T-S-O-N.
A. What is your email address?
    B. *My email address is* l_watson_19_74@hotmail.com
A. Okay, and what is your telephone number?
    B. *My telephone number is* 019-9734-4685.
A. Oh, Thank you.
    B. You're welcome.

Basic Interview

Exercise 5

BASIC INTERVIEW. Working in groups, interview your classmates by asking each other the following questions. While your partner asks you a question, try not to look at your book or read the question. Just listen to your partner's question and try to answer it without reading anything. You and your partner can time each interview to check if you're getting faster, but make sure you speak clearly. The example answers are A+ answers. Always try to give A+ answers, rather than short one-word answers. After practicing for a while, you and your partner should be able to ask and answer all eighteen questions in less than a minute.

그룹내의 친구들에게 될 수 있으면 책을 보지 말고 다음 문장들을 인터뷰 하세요. 대답할 때는 짧은 단어 하나보다는 주어진 예답처럼 완벽한 문장으로 답하세요.

1. How are you? *I'm fine thank you.*
2. Can you speak English? *Yes, I can speak English, a little.*
3. What's your name? *My name is . . . . .*
4. What's your first name/given name? *My . . . . . is . . . . .*
5. What's your last name/family name? *My . . . . is . . . . .*
6. Where are you from? *I'm from . . . .*
7. What's your hometown? *My hometown is . . . . .*
8. How old are you? *I'm . . . . . years old.*
9. When's your birthday? *My birthday is . . . . . .*
10. Where do you live? *I live in . . . . .*
11. What do you do? *I'm a . . . . .*
12. Are you married? *Yes, I'm married. (No, I'm not married.)* or *(No, I'm single.)*
13. What's your blood type? *My blood type is type . . . . .*
14. What's your major? *My major is . . . . .*
15. How do you spell your last name? *My last name is . . . . . .*
16. What's your email address? *My email address is . . . . . .*
17. What's your telephone number? *My telephone number is . . . . . .*
18. Which school do you go to? *I go to . . . . (I don't go to school)*

Interview by Zoethustra

Pronunciation

Exercise 6

REWRITING. **First**, rewrite the following questions and answers. **Then**, practice the conversation.
1번 예문처럼 먼저 문제와 답을 정확한 문장으로 다시 쓴 후에 대화를 연습하세요.

1. A. Where from you are? .... *Where are you from?* ....
2.   B. Seoul I'm from ....
3. A. Are married you? ....
4.   B. single, no I'm ....
5. A. What do do you? ....
6.   B. student a I'm ....
7. A. email address what's your? ....
8.   B. good_kimchi77@hanmail.net my address email is ....
9. A. live do you where? ....
10.   B: I Taejon live in ....

Exercise 7

PRONUNCIATION TIP: NUMBERS: When we speak English fluently, some numbers have a "Nee" or "Dee" sound. For example, "*twenty*", "*seventy*", "*forty*", and "*eighty*" sound like **"twen-nee, "seven-nee", "four-dee"**, and **"AD"**. We usually DON'T SAY "Twen-tee", "six-tee" etc.

The teens are pronounced slower than the above numbers. For example, *seven-nee* (70) is usually pronounced much quicker than *seven-teen* (17) *(*the stress is on *teen*.) When you speak English, especially when talking on the telephone, you should pronounce the teen numbers much slower than the other numbers to avoid confusion.

Now practice these:	Tee
	(None)
Nee	
20 (*Twen-nee*)	*Teeeen* (Here we have a "t"
70	sound)
90	
	13
	14
Dee	15
30 (*Thur-dee*)	16
40	17
50	18
60	19
80 *(AD)*	

Numbers

Exercise 8

IMPORTANT EXPRESSIONS: Here are some important words and expressions, which will help you to communicate in English. Please study and practice saying the expressions, which you are unfamiliar with.
다음 중요한 표현들을 공부하고 연습 하세요.

Are you okay? 괜찮아요?
Be careful! 조심하세요.
Because 왜냐하면
Can I help you? 도와드릴까요?
Can you help me please? 도와주시겠어요?
Can you repeat that please? 다시 한번반복 해주시겠어요?
Can you say that again please? 다시 한번 말씀해주시겠어요?
Don't worry 걱정하지 마세요.
Do you understand? 이해 하시겠어요?
Have a good day! 좋은 하루되세요.
How are you? 안녕하세요?
How do you say... in English? 영어로 ~ 를 어떻게 말하지요?
Hurry up please! 서두르세요.
I can ~ 할 수 있어요.
I can't ~ 할 수 없어요.
I don't understand. 잘 모르겠어요.
I'm fine. Thank you. 잘지내요. 고마워요.
I'm sick. 아프다
I'm sorry. 죄송해요.
I want a . . . . . ~를 원해요.
I want to go to the . . . . . ? ~에 가고 싶어요.
Just a minute please. 잠깐만 기다리세요.
Next time 다음에
No 아니요
No problem! 천만해요.
Last time 지난번

One more time please. 다시한번
Please stop! 멈추세요.
Sit down please. 앉으세요.
Stand up please. 일어 나세요.
Take your time. 천천히 하세요.
Thank you. 감사합니다.
That's okay. 괜찮아요.
This afternoon 오늘 우후
This morning 오늘 아침
This time 이번
Today 오늘
Tomorrow 내일
Tonight 오늘밤
What 무엇
What are you doing? 뭐하세요?
What does . . . . . mean? ~ 는 무엇을 의미 합니까?
What's this? 이것은 무엇입니까?
What time is it? 몇시예요?
What's wrong? 무슨 일 있으세요?
When . . . . . ? 언제?
Where is . . . . . ? 어디에?
Where is the . . . . . ? 어디에 ~ 이 있어요?
Who is he? 그는 누구입니까?
Why 왜요?
Yes 예
Yesterday 어제

Exercise 9

NUMBERS. Practice saying the following numbers (Continued on page 27):

13 *(Say it slowly)*	80	63	95	16
30 *(Say it quickly)*	90	71	18	27
14 *(Say it slowly)*	18	85	25	15
40 *(Say it quickly)*	19	89	68	84
16	24	19	15	46
60	13	90	26	35
17	30	97	14	60
70	49	34	64	16

Unit 2: Talking About You and Others

• **VOCABULARY**: Study these words and then practice saying them with your class.

About ~ 대한
Actor 배우
Actress 여배우
Alive 살아있는, 생생한
Architect 건축가
Aunt 숙모
Are you sleepy? 졸려요?
Are you tired? 피곤하세요?
Awake 깨어있는
Best friend 제일 친한 친구
Bored 지루한
CEO 최고 경영자
Christian 기독교인
Classmates 반친구
CM (centimeters) 센티미터
Comfortable 편안한
Cook 요리사
Cute 귀여운
Dead 돌아가신
Drinker 음주자
Exciting 재미있는
Expensive 비싼

Fat 뚱뚱한
Famous 유명한
Friend 친구
Friendly 친절한
Golfer 골퍼
Grandparents 조부모
Housewife 주부
Hungry 배고픈
Interesting 재미있는
Journalist 언론인
Kind 친절한
Large 큰
Late 늦은
Parent 부(모)
President 대통령
Puppy 강아지
Rainy 비오는
Related 관련있는
Skier 스키 타는 사람
Smoker 흡연자
Spicy 매운
Sports fan 스포츠 팬

Sports bar 스포츠 바
Spouse 배우자
Supervisor 감독자
Thin 마른

Dialogue

DIALOGUE 1. Again, with your class and in small groups, practice the following conversation. 다시 한번 다음 대화를 연습 하세요.

A. Are you hungry?
    B. No, I'm not hungry, but I'm thirsty.
    How about you, are you hungry?
A. Yes, I'm hungry.
    B. Are you thirsty?
A. Yes, I'm very thirsty.
    B. Then let's go to a sports bar.
A. Okay. That sounds great!

DIALOGUE 2. Again, with your class and in small groups, practice the following conversation.

A. Are you single?
    B. Yes, I'm single.
A. Are you <u>a</u> student?
    B. No, I'm not <u>a</u> student. I'm an engineer.
A. Wow! You look so young!
    B. Thanks. How about you, are you married?
A. Yes, I'm married. I'm an English teacher.
    B. An English teacher!
A. Yes, I'm <u>a</u> Korean-Canadian.
    B. Oh, I see. Is your wife <u>a</u> Canadian?
A. No, she's not <u>a</u> Canadian.
    B. Is she <u>a</u> teacher?
A. Hahaha! No, she's not <u>a</u> teacher. She's <u>a</u> housewife.

Interview

Exercise 3

INTERVIEW 1: ARE YOU? Ask your classmates the following questions. Take turns asking and then answering them with "**Yes, I am**", or "**No, I'm not**". 다음 문장들을 서로 질문하고 대답 하세요. 주어진 예답처럼 "Yes, I am" 또는 "No, I'm not" 이라고 답하세요. (Note: these are only C+ answers.)

1. Are you Korean? *Yes, I am.*
2. Are you sick? *No, I'm not.*
3. Are you tired?
4. . . . . . Chinese?
5. . . . . . you <u>a</u> golfer?
6. . . . . . happy now?
7. . . . . . <u>a</u> smoker?
8. . . . . . <u>a</u> sports fan?
9. . . . . . Christian?
10. . . . . . single?
11. . . . . . Moon Dae-sung?
12. . . . . . <u>a</u> good cook?

Exercise 4

INTERVIEW 2. In groups, ask your classmates the following questions. The example answers are A+ answers. If you hear "**a**" in the question, then "**a**" should be in your answer. If "**a**" is not in the question, then "**a**" should not be in the answer.
그룹내의 친구들과 다음 문장들을 연습 하세요. 질문에 "a" 가 있으면 대답 에도 있어야 합니다.

1. Are you Japanese? *No, I'm not Japanese*
2. Are you okay? *Yes, I'm okay.*
3. Are you <u>a</u> mother? *No, I'm not <u>a</u> mother.*
4. Are you <u>a</u> student?
5. Are you <u>a</u> teacher?
6. Are you <u>a</u> parent?
7. Are you <u>a</u> skier?
8. Are you Korean?
9. Are you busy?
10. . . . . . bored?
11. . . . . . sleepy?
12. . . . . . hungry?
13. . . . . . <u>a</u> CEO?
14. . . . . . cold?
15. . . . . . awake?
16. . . . . . thirsty?
17. . . . . . married?
18. . . . . . comfortable?
19. . . . . . <u>a</u> drinker?
20. . . . . . <u>a</u> supervisor?
21. . . . . . <u>a</u> good golfer?
22. . . . . ?
23. . . . . ?
24. . . . . ?

Golfer: by Arbron

Verb: BE

GRAMMAR REFRESHER. THE VERB "BE". **Study** the verb "be" and **then** try to do Exercise 5 below. "be" 동사를 공부하고, 아래 연습 문제를 풀어 보세요.

I am (I'm)   Aunt Martha (She's)
You are (You're)   Tiger Woods (He's)
She/He/It is (She's/He's/It's)   The Japanese (They're)
We are (We're)   The Koreans (We're)
They are (They're)   My computer (It's)
You are (You're)   My grandparents (They're)
Uncle Joe (He's)   Seoul (It's)

Exercise 5

BE. Complete the following sentences with the appropriate words from *GRAMMAR REFRESHER*, above.
1, 2번 예문처럼 위의 *GRAMMAR REFRESHER* 에서 알맞은 대명사 표현을 골라 문장을 완성 하세요.

1. My parents are on vacation in Europe. Right now . . . *they're* . .. in London.
2. My brother is very tall. He . . . *is*. . . . . 190 cm tall.
3. My grandmother is very sick . . *she's*. . . . in the hospital.
4. I love you because you . . . . very kind.
5. Kim Hee-sun has an excellent job. . . . . . an actress
6. My brother is working for Daewoo. He . . . . a computer programmer.
7. Don't go outside! . . . . too cold.
8. Roh Moo-hyun works in the Blue House. . . . . . . the president of South Korea.
9. We don't want to climb Puk'an Mountain because . . . . too tired.
10. Oh really, I thought you didn't want to climb the mountain because . . . . too lazy.
11. You . . . . a good student because you study very hard.
12. My grandparents are 87 years old. . . . . very old.
13. No, they . . . . not too old.
14. I can't go to the meeting because . . . . sick.
15. Seoul is the capital city . . . . very big.
16. Interestingly, Mokpo National University isn't in Mokpo . . . . . . in Chong-gye.

Bluehouse: by eimoberg

Famous People

FAMOUS PEOPLE

Park Ji-sung	**Bill Gates**
Occupation: Professional soccer player Soccer team: Manchester United Height: 175 cm tall Weight: 70 kg Hometown: Suwon, South Korea Date of Birth: February 25, 1981 Nick name: "Worker" Smoker: No!	Occupation: The chairman of Microsoft Hometown: Seattle, Washington Date of Birth: October 28, 1955 Marital Status: Married Hobbies: Golfing, reading and playing cards Smoker: No!
Avril Lavigne *(Sounds like "a-vro La-veen")* Occupation: Singer and songwriter Hometown: Napanee, Canada Height: 160 cm tall Place of Birth: Belleville, Canada Hobbies: Singing and skating Date of Birth: September 27, 1984 Marital Status: Married Smoker: Yes!	**Won Bin** Occupation: Actor Height: 178 cm tall Weight: 63 kg Religion: Christian Favorite color: Black Blood Type: O Hobbies: Taekwondo, skiing, computer games, basketball and photography Date of Birth: September 29, 1977 English nick name: Anthony

Exercise

INTERVIEW 3. Look at the list of FAMOUS PEOPLE above and ask each other the following questions.
위의 "FAMOUS PEOPLE" 내용을 보면서, 다음을 질문하고 대답 하세요.

1. Is Avril Lavigne a Canadian?
Yes, she is a Canadian.
2. Are Park Ji-Sung and Won Bin Korean?
Yes, they're Korean.
3. Is Bill Gates Korean?
No, he's not Korean.
4. Are Bill Gates and Avril Lavigne from Vancouver?
No, they are not from Vancouver.
5. Is Won Bin married?
I don't know if he is married.
6. Is Won Bin Christian?
7. Is Won Bin an actor?
8. Is Won Bin 200 cm tall?
9. Is Avril Lavigne married?
10. Is Avril Lavigne a singer?
11. Are Avril Lavigne and Bill Gates Spanish?
12. Is Avril Lavigne a smoker?
13. Is Park Ji-sung a smoker?
14. Is Park Ji-sung from Suwon?
15. Are Park Ji-sung and Won Bin 55 years old?
16. Is Bill Gates a smoker?
17. ....?
18. ....?

Interview

Exercise 7

INTERVIEW 4. With your class and in groups, ask each other the following questions. The A+ examples will help you answer them. Remember, if you hear "**a**" in the question, then "**a**" should be in your answer.
그룹내의 친구들과 다음을 연습 하세요. 질문에 "a"가 있으면 대답에도 있어야 합니다.

1. Is Boa Korean?
Yes, she's Korean
2. Is today rainy?
No, it's not rainy.
3. Are puppies cute?
Yes, they're cute.
4. Are Kim Richards and Kim Basinger Korean?
No, they're not Korean.
5. Is Kang Ta Christian?
I don't know if he's Christian.
6. How old is Su-mi's father?
I don't know how old he is.
7. Is today hot?
8. Is your father a journalist?
9. Is Pak Se-ri Japanese?
10. Is Kang Ta Christian?
I don't know if he's . . . .
11. Is your brother a student?
Yes, he is a student. (I don't have a brother.)
12. Is Je-Judo in Korea? *Yes, it's . . . . .*
13. Are dogs friendly?
Yes, they're . . . . . .
14. Are Brazilians good soccer players?
15. Is Rain (Bi) a bad singer?
16. Is Jackie Chan Korean?
17. Are Korean women beautiful?
Yes, they're . . . . . .
18. Is this English class exciting?
19. Are Koreans thin? *Yes, they're . . . .*
20. Are Koreans friendly?
21. Is Japan expensive? *Yes, it is . . . . .*
22. Are Bill Clinton and Hillary Clinton related? *Yes, they're . . . . .*
23. Is Park Sin-yang a good actor?
24. . . . . . Ha Ri-soo a woman?
25. . . . . . Lee Mi-yeon a good actress?
26. . . . . . Chiri a good movie?
27. . . . . . Silmido a sad movie?
28. . . . . . Spiderman a sad movie?

Spiderman: by Janex

Questions

Exercise 8

MAKE QUESTIONS. For each of the following answers, write a question. For assistance, look at the questions in exercises 1-7 above.
각각의 대답이 나올 수 있도록 알맞은 질문을 만드세요. 위의 exercises 1-7를 참고 하세요.

1. No, I'm not an architect . . . . *Are you an architect?*
2. Yes, it's cold. It's very cold! . . . . *Is it cold?*
3. Yes, I'm a soccer fan . . . .
4. No, he's not a good cook . . . . *Is he a good cook?*
5. Yes, Korean women are beautiful . . . .
6. Yes, it's a great movie. . . . .
7. No, today is not rainy. . . . .
8. No, she is not married. She's single . . . .
9. Yes, he's a smoker. . . . .
10. Yes, I am a good snowboarder. . . . .
11. No, Jackie Chan is not Korean. . . . .
12. Yes, *Silmido* is a sad movie. . . . .

Snowboarder: by Yommtde

More Famous People

MORE FAMOUS PEOPLE (And your mom)

	Place of Birth	Date of Birth	Occupation (Job)
1. Kang Ta	South Korea	October 10, 1979	Singer
2. Tom Cruise	The U.S.	July 3, 1962	Actor
3. Park Chan-ho	South Korea	June 30, 1973	Baseball player
4. Banana Yoshimoto	Japan	July 25, 1964	Writer
5. Pak Se-ri	South Korea	September 28, 1977	Golfer
6. Mel Gibson	Australia	January 3, 1956	Actor
7. Leonardo DiCaprio	The U.S.	November 11, 1974	Actor
8. Celine Dion	Canada	March 30, 1965	Singer
9. Your mom			

Exercise 9

INTERVIEW 5. As in the above exercises, interview your classmates by asking each other the following questions. When answering them, try not to read, but rather, listen to the questions. (Note if you are the teacher, you can put the students into small circles and do this as a chain exercise.)
위에서 연습 했던 것처럼, 될 수 있으면 책을 보지 말고 다음 문장들을 서로 인터뷰 하세요.

1. What's your mom's name?
Her name is In-hee.
(or "My mom's name is In-hee")
2. Where is Celine Dion from?
She's from Canada.
3. Where is Tom Cruise from?
He's from the U.S.
4. Where are Tom Cruise and Leonardo DiCaprio from? (*They're from . . . . . .*)
5. Where are Park Chan-ho and Pak Se-ri from?
6. Where is Celine Dion from?
7. Where's Mel Gibson from?
8. How old is your mom?
(*She's . . . . . . years old.*)

9. How old is Park Chan-ho?
10. How old is Kang Ta?
11. . . . . . . old is Mel Gibson?
12. . . . . . . old is Leonardo DiCaprio?
13. What does Pak Se-ri do? (*She's a . . .*)
14. . . . . does your mother do? (*She's a . . .*)
15. What do Kang Ta and Celine Dion do?
16. . . . . Park Chan-ho do?
17. . . . . Banana Yoshimoto do?
18. Where is Banana Yoshimoto from?
19. Where's your mom from?
20. Where's Leonardo DiCaprio from?
21. . . . . your English teacher from?

Numbers

PRONUNCIATION TIP: NUMBERS: When people speak English fluently, "and" usually sounds like "in". 247 is "two hundred and forty seven", but when we speak fluently, "and" sounds like "**in**" and 247 sounds like "two hundred *in* forty seven".
영어를 유창하게 빨리 말하면 "and" 발음이 마치 "in" 처럼 들립니다. 다음 숫자들을 연습하세요.

Exercise 10

NUMBERS: Now practice saying the following (Continued on page 63):

1. 249 (*Two-hundred in forty-nine*)
2. 386 (*Three-hundred in eighty-six*)
3. 586
4. 200
5. 213
6. 230
7. 392
8. 639
9. 519
10. 590
11. 983
12. 415
13. 450
14. 800
15. 852
16. 173
17. 117
18. 170
19. 357
20. 717
21. 770

Exercise 11

YEARS. We say years differently than the way we say numbers. Practice saying the following in the same way that they're shown in the examples.
연도 읽는 방법은 숫자 읽는 방법과 다릅니다. 예문을 보면서 연습하세요.

1. 1600 (***Six****teen hundred*)
2. 1605 (***Six****teen Oh-five*)
3. 1609 (***Six****teen Oh-nine*)
4. 1616 (***Six****teen Six****teeen***)
5. 1660 (***Six****teen **Six**-D*)
6. 1700
7. 1703
8. 1707
9. 1717
10. 1770 (***Sev****inteen **Sev****inee*)
11. 1800
12. 1809
13. 1818
14. 1880
15. 1900
16. 1903
17. 1907
18. 1917
19. 1967
20. 1976
21. 1990
22. 1999
23. 2000 (*Too-**thow**-zind*)
24. 2001 (*Too-**thow**-zin-in-won*)
25. 2002 (*Too-**thow**-zin-in too*)
26. 2003
27. 2004
28. 2005
29. 2006
30. 2007
31. 2008
32. 1950's (*the **nine**teen fifties*)
33. 1960's
34. 1970's
35. 1980's
36. 1990's

Pronunciation

Exercise 12

PRONUNCIATION. First, study the pronunciation of the following words. The emphasis is in bold. Second, listen as your teacher pronounces each word. Third, practice saying them with the entire class.
먼저 단어의 발음을 공부 하세요. 선생님의 발음을 잘 들은 후에 볼드체 부분을 강조하면서 다 같이 읽어 보세요.

1. Air Conditioning (**Air** cun-di-shin-ning)
2. Always (**All**-weez)
3. American (A-**mair**-rih-kin)
4. Basketball (**Bass**-kit-ball)
5. Bicycle (**Bye**-sih-koe)
6. Canuck (Ka-**nuck**) or (Kin-**nuck**)
7. Chicago (Shih-**Kah**-go)
8. Chocolate (**Chaw**-klit)
9. Clinton (**Klin**-tin)
10. Computer (Cum-**pew**-der)
11. Delicious (D-**lish**-siss)
12. Dishes (**Dih**-shiz) or (**Dish**-iz)
13. Easiest (**E**-zee-ist)
14. Egypt (**E**-jipt)
15. Elephant (**El**-li-fint)
16. Engineer (In-jin-**eer**)
17. Exercise (**Eck**-sir-size)
18. Exercises (**X**-sir-sigh-ziz)
19. Friends (**Frenz**)
20. Handsome (**Han**-sim) or (**Han**-sum)
21. Kangaroo (**Kang**-ga-roo)
22. Manage (**Ma**-nij)
23. Monopoly (Mah-**nawp**-poe-lee)
24. Office (**Aw**-fiss)
25. Ottawa (**Aw**-duh-waw) or (**Aw**-dah-waw)
26. Parent (**Pair**-rint)
27. Regularly (**Reg**-gyu-lair-lee)
28. Robert (**Raw**-burt)
29. Snake (**Snaik**)
30. Spaghetti (Spih-**ggeh**-D)
31. Thai (**Tie**)
32. Vacation (Vay-**kay**-shin)
33. University (U-ni-**ver**-si-D)
34. Weekend (**Wee**-Kend)
35. Winnipeg (**Win**-nih-peg)

Exercise: by Mike Baird

28

Unit 3: Do, Doing, and Other Verbs

• **VOCABULARY**: Study these words and then practice saying them with your class.

Air conditioning 에어컨
Alcohol 술
Always 항상
Beer 맥주
Best friend 제일 친한 친구
Bicycle 자전거
God 신
Candy 사탕
Canuck 프랑스계 캐나나인
Children 어린이들
Chocolate 쵸콜렛
Country 나라
Church 교회
Delicious 맛있는
Desks 책상들
"Do the dishes" 요리하다
Easiest 가장 쉬운
Engineer 기술자
Elephant 코끼리
Grandmother 할머니
Grandparents 조부모님
Job 직업

Just 막
Healthy 건강한
Handsome 잘생긴
Housework 집안일
Kangaroo 캥거루
Library 도서관
Manager 매니저
Many things 많은것들
Monopoly   (Boardgame)
모노폴리 (게임이름)
Mountain 산
Morning 아침
Office 사무실
Ottawa 오타와 (캐나다 수도)
Push-ups 엎드려 팔굽혀 펴기
Rain 비
Regularly 규칙적으로
Russians 러시아인들
Sick 아픈
Snake 뱀
Spanish 스페인어
Spicy 매운

Subway 지하철
Thai 타이
Tired 피곤한
Two months ago 두달전에
Vacation 휴가
Want 원하다
Winnipeg   위니펙   (캐나다
Manitoba 주의 주도)

Dialogue

MORE VOCABULARY: (VERBS): Study and practice saying the following verbs.

"Believe in" 믿다
"Brush your teeth" 양치질하다
Clean 청소하다
Climb 등산하다
Collect stamps 우표수집하다
Cook 요리하다
Do ~하다
"Do the dishes" 요리하다
Drink 마시다
Enjoy 즐기다
Exercise 운동하다

Feel sick 아프다
Fly 날다
Hate 미워하다
Help 돕다
Lift weights 역도
Look tired 피곤해 보이다
Move to ~로 이사하다
Mountain climbing 등산
Need 필요하다
Rain 비오다
Ride 타다

Sell 팔다
Sing 노래하다
Smoke 담배피다
"Stay home" 집에 있다
"Take care of" 돌보다
Try 시도하다
Wait 기다리다
Walk 걷다
"Watch baseball" 야구보다
Worry 걱정하다

Exercise 1

DIALOGUE. Practice this conversation. Please refer to this dialogue to assist you with future exercises in this textbook.
다음 대화를 연습하고, 앞으로 연습 문제를 공부할 때 참고 하세요.

A. Do you live/work here in Taejon?
    B. No, I don't. I live in Suwon.
A. Oh really! Do you work for Samsung?
    B. Yes, I do.
A. What do you do there?
    B. I'm an engineer/a manager.
A. Do you like Suwon?
    B. Yes, I love Suwon.
A. Do you have many friends in Suwon?
    B. No, I don't. I just moved there two months ago.
A. Does your wife like Suwon?
    B. Yes, she does. She loves it.
A. Does she work too?
    B. No, she doesn't work. She stays home and takes care of the children.

Do/Does

GRAMMAR 1: DO. Study the following examples.

I do	For example: **I do** push-ups every day.
You do	For example: **You do** your homework in the library.
He **does**	For example: **He does** his homework in the library.
She **does**	For example: After she eats, **she** always **does** the dishes.
Does she	For example: **Does she** like children?
It **does**	For example: **It does** not have a camera.
We do	For example: **We** usually **do** the easiest questions first.
They do	For example: **They do** their work in the office.

Exercise

DO/DOES. Complete the following expressions with **do** or **does**. (This can be a written exercise or done orally with the whole class.)
다음 표현들을 do나 does를 넣어 완성 하세요.

1. I .do......
2. They .....
3. We ......
4. She ......
5. You ......
6. It ....
7. He ......
8. They .....
9. Sim Eun-ha .....
10. Tom and Jerry .....
11. The Russians ......
12. My computer ......
13. My wife ....
14. The tree ....
15. My children ....
16. The teachers ......
17. Jim Carrey ....
18. The desks ....
19. My friends ....
20. Cats ....
21. My dog ....

Do/Does

Exercise 3

DO/DOES 2. Fill in the blanks with **do** or **does**.

1. What do you . . . *do* . . ?
2. Where . . . . you live?
3. What . . . . Robert do?
4. . . . . your mother like spaghetti?
5. When . . . . you go to school?
6. . . . . your computer have Internet?
7. We . . . . . our homework in the library.
8. Many people . . . . . . not like Thai food.
9. My sister . . . . a good job.
10. I . . . . my homework on the computer.
11. Bob . . . . . his exercise in the morning.
12. After dinner, TJ and Rob. . . . . . . .the dishes.

GRAMMAR 2: DO NOT. Again, study the following examples and then do Exercise 4 below.
다음 예문들을 공부하고 밑에 있는 Exercise 4를 풀어 보세요.

Do Not…..
I do not (**don't**)   For example: **I don't** speak Chinese.
You do not (**don't**)   For example: **You don't** live in Kwangju.
She does not (**doesn't**)   For example: **She doesn't** smoke.
He does not (**doesn't**)   For example: **He doesn't** like spicy food.
It does not (**doesn't**)   For example: **It doesn't** look cold.
We do not (**don't**)   For example: **We don't** want it to rain.
They do not (**don't**)   For example: **They don't** play StarCraft.

Playing Starcraft: by cplbasilisk

32

Don't/Doesn't

DON'T/DOESN'T. Fill in the blanks with **don't** or **doesn't**.

1. I .. *don't*. . . . like alcohol.
2. I . . . . go to church.
3. We . . . . drink beer.
4. She . . . . have a computer.
5. Tara and Pardeep . . . . . live in Korea.
6. My wife . . . . speak English.
7. Most Koreans . . . . . like George Bush.
8. You . . . . look tired.
9. . . . . you swim?
10. Why . . . . you exercise?
11. Most Koreans . . . . play hockey.
12. Most Americans . . . . . . watch hockey.
13. My grandmother . . . . work.
14. My friends . . . . like night clubs.
15. My grandmother . . . . smoke.
16. Brad Pitt . . . . live in London.

DO/DOESN'T. Again, fill in the blanks. This time use **do, don't, does** or **doesn't**.
다음 빈칸에 do, don't, does 또는 doesn't를 넣어 문장을 완성 하세요.

1. My sister isn't married and she . . . *doesn't*. . .have a boyfriend.
2. What do you want to . . . *do* . . . ?
3. No, she . . . . live in Inchon.
4. I . . . . .like kimchi because it's too spicy
5. We . . . . . want to walk. We're too tired.
6. . . . . Ji-sun live in Taejon?
7. . . . . he work in Ottawa?
8. He's very healthy. He exercises and he . . . . drink or smoke.
9. . . . . it snow in Chicago?
10. There are many things they like to . . . . during the vacation.
11. Most Korean women . . . . smoke.
12. If we . . . . a good job, they'll pay us lots of money.
13. She . . . . look happy. Maybe she's sad.
14. When he tries, he . . . . a good job.
15. Yes, she always . . . . . her homework.
16. Yes, I . . . . my housework in the morning.
17. I have to . . . . the dishes.
18. Park ji-sung . . . . smoke.
19. I . . . . clean the apartment because my wife does it.

Interview

Exercise 6

INTERVIEW 1. Interview your classmates by asking each other the following questions. Answer them by using "**Yes, I do**" or "**No, I don't**" (Note: In this exercise, you are only required to give C+ answers) 다음 문장들을 서로 질문하고 대답하세요. 주어진 예답처럼, "Yes, I do" 또는 "No, I don't" 라고 답하세요.

1. Do you live in Daegu? *Yes I do. (No, I don't.)*
2. Do you climb mountains? *No, I don't. (Yes, I do.)*
3. Do you speak English?
4. Do you live in Osan?
5. Do you cook?
6. Do you go to school?
7. . . . . . you live in Yong-in?
8. . . . . . you like soccer?
9. . . . . . like Roh Moo-hyun?
10. . . . . . play tennis?
11. . . . . . watch baseball?
12. . . . . . smoke?
13. . . . . . enjoy movies?
14. . . . . . want a vacation?

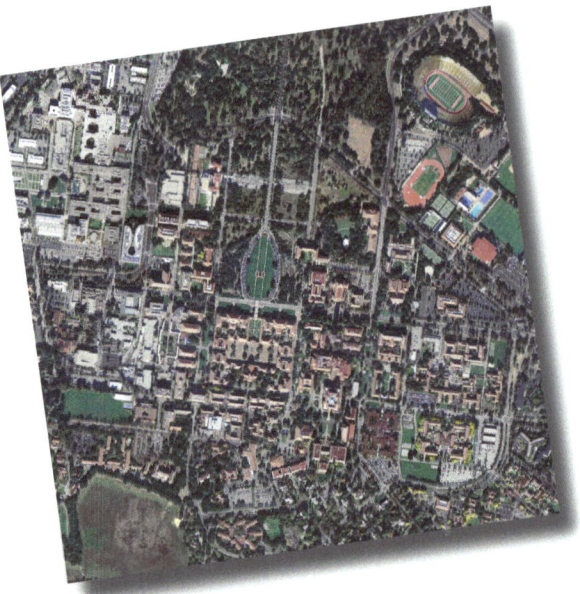

GRAMMAR 3: PRESENT VERBS. When using verbs in the present tense, we normally add an "**s**" to the end of the verb for "**he**", "**she**" and "**it**". Study and then practice saying these together with your class. 주어가 "he," "she," 또는 "it" 인 경우, 동사 뒤에 보통 "**s**"를 붙입니다. 다음 예문들을 보면서 연습하세요.

EXAMPLE 1: *PLAY*

I play
You play
He play**s**
She play**s**
It play**s**
They play
We play
My sister . . . .

EXAMPLE 2: *LIKE*

I like
you like
He like**s**

She like**s**
It like**s**
They like
We like
The Americans . . . .

EXAMPLE 3: *GO*

I go
You go
He goe**s**
She goe**s**
It goe**s**
They go
We go
My wife . . . .

EXAMPLE 4: *DRINK*

I drink
You drink
He drink**s**
She drink**s**
It drink**s**
They drink
We drink
The horse . . . .

Where do you live: by Peter Kaminsky

Play

Exercise 7

PLAY. Fill in the blanks with the proper form of the verb, "**play**". Remember, Michelle Wie is a "she" and children are "they".
동사 "play" 의 알맞은 형태를 쓰세요. Michelle Wie는 "she"로 받고 children은 "they"로 받습니다.

1. I ...*play*... soccer.
2. He .. *plays*..... baseball.
3. They .... basketball.
4. We .... volleyball.
5. You .... computer games.
6. Michelle Wie .... golf.
7. My friends .... soccer.
8. My father .... golf.
9. My children .... computer games.
10. My aunt .... *Go-Stop*.
11. My students .... *Monopoly*.
12. David Beckham .... soccer.
13. The Japanese .... baseball.
14. The Vancouver Canucks .... ice-hockey.
15. Steve Nash .... basketball.

Exercise 8

PRESENT TENSE VERBS. Fill in the blanks with the proper verb and the proper form of the verb. Choose your answers from the following list:
빈 칸에 알맞은 동사를 보기에서 골라 문장을 완성 하세요. 필요한 경우 1번처럼 동사 형태를 바꾸세요.

> cook   ride   love   sing   go   drink   drink   play
> work   watch   listen   hate   speak   read

1. He ...*rides*.... his bicycle.
2. She .... Pepsi.
3. Grandmother .... spaghetti very well.
4. I .... English.
5. She .... to church.
6. Canadians .... hockey.
7. On weekends, we .... movies.
8. On Fridays, we .... soju.
9. I .... George Bush.
10. She .... Johnny Depp.
11. My children always .... comics.
12. Ji-sook .... to her MP3 player.
13. Yeong-min .... for SK Telecom.
14. Jo Sung-mo .... well.

Interview

Exercise 9

DOESN'T. Fill in the blanks with "**don't**" or "**doesn't**" and a proper verb. In this situation, **you don't need an "s"** at the end of the verb.
"don't" 또는 "doesn't" 을 넣어 문장을 완성 하세요. 이 경우에는 동사 뒤에 "s" 가 필요하지 않습니다.

1. My brother ..*doesn't eat*.. fish.
2. Africans .. *don't play* .. hockey.
3. This computer .. *doesn't have* .. iTunes.
4. Elephants ... *don't have* ... hair.
5. Egypt . . . . snow.
6. Hyun-jin . . . . soccer.
7. Kangaroos . . . . in Korea.
8. I . . . . any money.
9. She . . . . beer.
10. Mom . . . . English.
11. Kangaroos . . . . TV.
12. Snakes . . . . legs.
13. My room . . . . air conditioning
14. They . . . . to music.

Exercise 10

INTERVIEW 2. Again, interview your classmates.

1. Do you work? *Yes, I work.*
2. Do you feel sick? *No, I don't feel sick.*
3. Do you drink beer? *Yes, I drink beer.*
4. Do you like cooking?
5. Do you play soccer?
6. Do you have a sister?
7. . . . . . go to church?
8. . . . . . you enjoy singing?
9. . . . . . you speak Chinese?
10. . . . . . play StarCraft?
11. . . . . . believe in God?
12. . . . . . like Naju Pears?
13. . . . . . go to university?
14. . . . . . like Choi Ji-woo?
15. . . . . . always eat Korean food?
16. . . . . . watch TV every day?
17. . . . . . watch KBL basketball?
18. . . . . . take a shower every day?
19. . . . . . always stay home on Sunday?
20. . . . . . think today is cold? *Yes, I think today is cold.*
21. . . . . . think Tom Cruise is handsome?
22. . . . . . think chocolate is delicious?
23. . . . . . Rain (Bi) is a good singer?
24. What are five things you do every day?

Interview

Exercise 11

INTERVIEW 3. (Note: Here, you only need to give C+ answers)

1. Does your mother use the Internet?
No, she doesn't. (or, "my mother died")
2. Does your mother speak Korean?
Yes, she does.
3. Do your friends study English?
No, they don't.
4. Does your mother speak English?
5. . . . . mother cook spaghetti?
6. Does Kim Jeong-Ill live in Seoul?
7. Does Spiderman speak English?
8. Does your best friend speak English?
9. . . . your computer have a web cam?
10. Do Kangaroos live in Australia?
11. Does David Beckham play hockey?
12. Do Koreans like spicy food?
13. . . . . . children like candy?
14. Does your mother like Choi Ji-woo?
15. Do your parents live in Australia?
16. Does Incheon have a subway?

Hockey: by KamalSell

Accent Reduction

Exercise

DOES/DO. Ask and answer questions about the following images. As in the examples, try to give A+ answers.
각각의 그림들을 보면서 다음 문장들을 서로 연습 하세요.

1. Q: Does it fly?
   A: *No, it doesn't fly.*
2. Q: Do they read?
   A: *Yes, they read.*
3. Does she cook?
4. Do they study?
5. . . . . he drink beer?
6. . . . . . . play golf?
7. . . . . .she walk?
8. . . . . bathe?
9. . . . . . . .brush his teeth?
10. . . . . she sell hotdogs?
11. . . . . drive a car?
12. . . . . .walk fast?

ACCENT REDUCTION TIP: "i" SOUND. When most Canadians and Americans speak English, the last syllable of each word usually has an "i" sound. It sounds like "*shin*", "*pin*", "*tin*", "*tint*", "*mint*", "*iss*" and so on. Here are some examples: (Note 1: The stress is in bold.) (Note 2: the italicized words are new words.)

Appointment (A-**point**-mint)
Assistant (A-**sis**-tint)
Christian (**Crish**-tin)
Dangerous (**Dain**-Jriss)
Delicious (D-**lish**'iss)
Excellent (**X**-lint or **X**-sil'int)
Favorite (**Faiv**-rit)

Important (Im-**por**-tint)
Island (**Eye**-lind)
Mountain (**Moun**-tin)
Nervous (**Ner**-viss)
Parent (**Pair**-rint)
President (**Prez**-zi-dint)

Pronunciation

PRONUNCIATION TIP: SILENT SYLLABLES. Note some words have four syllables, but only three syllables are pronounced. Other words have three syllables but only two syllables are pronounced. Here are some examples:

*Evening (**Eev**-ning)*
*Family (**Fam**-lee)*
*Favorite (**Faiv**-rit)*
*Camera (**Cam**-rah)*
*Chocolate (**Chaw**-klit)*

Comfortable (**Cumf**-der-boe)
History (**His**-tree)
Interesting (**In**-triss-ding)
Vegetable (**Vej**-tih-bowl)
Excellent (**X**-lint)

PRONUNCIATION. Listen to your teacher say the following words and then practice saying them with your class.

1. Address (*a-driss*) (*a-jriss*)
2. Bathe (verb) (B*aith*)
3. Climb (*Clime*)
4. Go to church (***Go**-dew-cherch*)
5. Go to movies (***Go**-dew-moo-veez*)
6. Jog (*Jawg*)
7. Last name (***Lass**-naim*)
8. Listen (***Liss**-sin*)
9. Mexican (***Meck**-sih-kin*)
10. Thousand (***Thow**-zin*) (***Thow**-zind*)
11. Vacuum (***Va**-Kyuum*) (***Va**-Quum*)

CUMULATIVE REVIEW. Practice the following review questions.

1. What is your given name?
2. Are you Korean?
3. Are you a good singer?
4. Is Bill Gates Korean?
5. Is Dokdo in Korea?
6. How old is Park Ji-sung?
7. Are Korean women pretty?
8. Where are Tom Cruise and Tom Hanks from?
9. Do you live in Gangnam?
10. Is *Gladiator* a sad movie?

Unit 4: Do, Doing, and Other Verbs 2

• **VOCABULARY**: Study and practice saying the following words.

Afternoon 오후
Every 모든
Morning 아침
Nick name 별명
Nurse 간호사
Sick 아픈
Sister 자매
Ten thousand 만원
Then 그리고 나서
Vacuum 청소기로 청소하다

Dialogue

MORE VOCABULARY: (VERBS): Study and practice saying the following verbs.

Bath 목욕
Take a bath 목욕하다
Crawl 기어가다
Drive 운전하다
Hike 하이킹하다
Jog 조깅하다
"Go out with my friends"
친구들과 외출하다
Listen 듣다
Meet 만나다

Read 읽다
Ride a bicycle 자전거 타다
Rock Climbing 암벽등반
Run 달리다
Sell hotdogs 핫도그를 팔다
Sing 노래하다
Sleep 자다
Sweep 청소하다
"Take a shower" 샤워하다
Think 생각하다

Vacuum the carpet 청소기로 청소하다
Visit 방문하다

Exercise 1

DIALOGUE. Practice this conversation. Please refer to this dialogue to assist you with future exercises in this textbook.
다음 대화를 연습하고, 앞으로 연습 문제를 공부할 때 참고 하세요.

A: Let's go golfing!
    B: I'm sorry I don't golf. Why don't you ask Hyun-jun?
A: Does Hyun-Jun play golf?
    B: Yes, he does.
A: Where does he play?
    B: *He* play**s** everywhere.
A: Can he play on Saturday?
    B: On Saturday, *he* work**s** and then goe**s** out with his friends.
A: And Sunday?
    B: On Sunday, *he* goe**s** to church, visit**s** his grandparents, and then watche**s** movies.
A: Well, when does he go golfing?
    B: *He* usually goe**s** golfing on Wednesday morning.
A: I see.

Interview

INTERVIEW 1. As in the examples, please give A+ answers.

1. Does your father speak Japanese?
No, he doesn't speak Japanese.
2. Does Bill Clinton live in the U.S.?
*Yes, he live**s** in the U.S.*
3. Do children go to school?
Yes, they go to school.
4. . . *Does* . . your mother cook Korean food?
5. . . . . . your mother live in Seoul?
6. . . . . . your English teacher live in Seoul?
7. . . . . . . Spiderman speak Korean?
8. . . . . . . your computer have Internet?
9. Do most Canadians speak Korean?
10. Do Johnny Depp and Brad Pitt act?
11. . . . . . . Mexicans speak Spanish?
12. . . *Do* . . children like to play?
13. . . . . . . Lee Hyo-ri sing well?
14. . . . . . . Michelle Wie play golf?
15. . . *Does* . . Park Chan-ho speak Korean?
16. . . . . . . nurses help sick people?
17. . . . . . .your mother drink green tea?
18. . . *Do* . Koreans like Dwenjang-jigae?
19. . . . . . . children drink soju?

WRITING QUESTIONS.

1. . . . . . *Does your brother live in Seoul.* . . . . ? Yes, my brother lives in Seoul.
2. . . . . ? Yes, my sister lives in Andong.
3. . . . .? Yes, my friend speaks English.
4. . . . . ? No, they don't sing well.
5. . . . .? No, Kim Hee-sun doesn't work in Africa.
6. . . . .? Yes, grandfather lives in Winnipeg.
7. . . . . ? Yes. So-ra lives in Pusan.
8. . . . .? Yes, John smokes.
9. . . . . ? Yes, she cooks well.
10. . . . . ? No, I don't speak German.

Schedule

Exercise 4

PARDEEP'S SCHEDULE. Study Pardeep's schedule. Then ask each other questions. Pay close attention to examples 8 and 12. You only need to use **and** once in each sentence.

Pardeep의 스케줄을 읽고 난 후에 다음 문장들을 서로 연습 하세요. 8번과 12번에 있는 예답 처럼 한 문장에 *and*를 한번만 사용 하는 것에 유의 하세요.

1. Does Pardeep go to work?
No, Pardeep/he doesn't go to work.
2. Does Pardeep play sports?
Yes, Pardeep plays sports.
3. Does Pardeep study Japanese?
4. . . . . Pardeep go to movies?
5. . . . . Pardeep visit his grandfather?
6. . . . . play basketball?
7. . . . . play golf
8. What does Pardeep do on Sunday morning? *On Sunday morning, he goes to church, and then plays soccer.*
9. What . . . . Pardeep do on Monday morning? *On Monday morning, Pardeep goes to school.*
10. .What . . . . Pardeep do on Tuesday evening?
11. . . . . .Pardeep do on Wednesday evening?
12. . . . . on Thursday? *On Thursday, he goes to school, swims, studies, and then reads.*
13. . . . . on Friday?
14. . . . . on Saturday afternoon?
15. When does Pardeep visit his grandmother? *Pardeep visits his grandmother on Sunday afternoon.*
17. . . . . go jogging? *Pardeep goes jogging on Monday, Wednesday and Friday.*
16. When does Pardeep study English? *He studies English on Monday and Wednesday evenings.*
18. . . . . read?
19. . . . . go to movies?

PARDEEP'S WEEKLY SCHEDULE

	Sunday	Monday	Tuesday	Wednesday	Thursday	Friday	Saturday
Morning.	Go to church	Go to school	Go to school	Go to school	Go to school	Go to school	Go to ABC English Academy
Morning	Play soccer						
Afternoon	Visit Grandmother				Swim		Play golf
Afternoon.		Study	Study	Study	Study	Study	
Evening		Go jogging	Listen to music	Go jogging		Go jogging	
Evening	Watch movies	Study English	Watch TV	Study English	Read	Meet his friends	Go to movies

Doing

Exercise 5

DOING. For each picture, ask each other what **he, she, it** or **they** are doing. Use the following list of verbs and collocations to help you answer your questions.
다음 그림들을 보면서 예시된 대화처럼 질문 하세요. 대답할 때 아래의 동사 표현들을 참고 하세요.

doing the dishes	hiking
skating	sleeping
playing basketball	sweeping
playing hockey	taking a shower
playing soccer	talking
reading	vacuuming

EXAMPLES:

1. A: What's he doing?
   B: *He's sleeping*
2. A: What are they doing?
   B: *They're skating.*

Writing Questions

Exercise 6

WRITING QUESTIONS 2. For each of the following, write a question. Later, ask your classmates the same questions.

1. Yes, I'm a nurse. . . . . *Are you a nurse?* . . . .
2. Yes, children like candy . . . .
3. No, I don't have an English nickname. . . . .
4. Yes, Spiderman speaks English. . . . .
5. No, I don't have ten thousand won. . . . .
6. No, kangaroos don't live in Russia. . . . .
7. I'm 57 years old. . . . .
8. No, I don't have any children . . . .
9. Yes, Korean women are beautiful. . . . .

Exercise 7

NUMERICAL ORDER. With your class, practice saying each of the following.

1. 1st – first
2. 2nd – second
3. 3rd – third
4. 4th – fourth
5. 5th – fifth
6. 7th – seventh
7. 9th – ninth
8. 11th – eleventh
9. 12th – twelfth
10. 13th – thirteenth
11. 15th – fifteenth
12. 16th – sixteenth
13. 18th – eighteenth
14. 20th – twentieth
15. 21st – twenty-first
16. 22nd - twenty-second
17. 23rd - twenty-third
18. 25th – twenty-fifth
19. 29th – twenty-ninth
20. 30th – thirtieth
21. 31st – thirty-first
22. 32nd - thirty-second
23. 33rd – thirty-third
24. 38th – thirty-eighth
25. 40th – fortieth
26. 42nd – forty-second
27. 50th – fiftieth
28. 63rd – sixty-third
29. 70th – seventieth
30. 81st – eighty-first
31. 94th – ninety-fourth
32. 100th – one hundredth
33. 101st – one hundred and first
34. 129th - one hundred and twenty ninth
35. 247th – Two hundred and forty seventh

Accent Reduction

Exercise 8

ACCENT REDUCTION. With your class, practice saying the following:

1. Architect (**Ar**-kih-tekt)
2. Athlete (**Ath**-leet)
3. Cigarette (**Sih**-gur-rett)
4. Clothes (*cloze*)
5. Country (**Cun**-tree)
6. Cousin (**Cuh**-zin)
7. Dictionary (**Dik**-shin-air-ree)
8. Digital camera (**Dih**-gi-doe cam-rah)
9. Dormitory (**Dorm**-mi-toar-ree)
10. Enough (*E-**nuff***)
11. Equator (*Eee-**Qway**-der*)
12. Foreign (**For**-rin)
13. Germany (**Ger**-min-nee)
14. Grandparents (**Grand**-pair-rints)
15. Handsome (**Han**-sim or **Han**-sum)
16. Important (Im-**por**-tint)
17. Island (**I**-lind)
18. License (**Lie**-sinz)
19. Listen (**Lis**-sin)
20. Novel (**Naw**-voe)
21. Nuclear weapon (**New**'klee-er wep'in)
22. Pocket (**Paw**-kit)
23. Skater (**Skay**-der)
24. Square (*Squair*)
25. Thousand (**Thow**-zind)
26. Triangle (**Try**-ang-go)
27. Weapon (**Wep**'in)
28. Work (*Werk*)
29. Zero (**Zee**-roe)

Exercise 9

CUMULATIVE REVIEW. Practice the following review questions.

1. How do you spell your last name?
2. What's your email address?
3. Are you sleepy?
4. Are you a sports fan?
5. Is Avril Lavigne Japanese?
6. Is Park Ji-sung a baseball player?
7. Are Park-Ji-sung and Won Bin Chinese?
8. Is today hot?
9. What does Leonardo DiCaprio do?
10. Do you drink green tea?
11. Does Roe Moo-hyun live in South Korea?
12. Do Mexicans speak English?
13. Does Pardeep go to school?

Game

Exercise 10

GAME. Working alone, or with your team (each team member taking turns to speak), try to say what each of the following people are doing. The fastest team is the winner. Each team or participant should be able to accomplish this exercise in under a minute. Each mistake is a two second penalty!

START

1. She's sweeping
2. He's sleeping
3. He's rock climbing
4. He's swimming
5. She's taking a shower
6. He's playing golf
7. He's cooking
8. He's reading the newspaper
9. He's vacuuming
10. She's playing soccer
11. He's playing baseball
12. He's drinking beer
13. She's riding her bicycle
14. They're smoking
15. He's watching TV
16. They're going to school
17. She's listening to music
18. They're studying
19. She's jogging
20. He's driving a truck
21. He's drinking coffee
22. They're getting married
23. They're shopping
24. He's brushing his teeth
25. She's crawling

Unit 5: More Verbs

• **VOCABULARY:** Again, study and practice saying the following words.
다음 단어를 연습 하세요.

Architect 건축가
Boots 부츠
Both 둘다
Carpet 카펫트
Cigarettes 담배
Clothes 옷
Cook 요리사
Country 나라
Cousin 사촌
Dormitory 기숙사
Driver's license 운전면허증
Floor 층
Free time 여가시간
Germany 독일
History 역사
Hole 구멍
Housewife 주부
Handsome 잘생긴
License 면허증
Meal 식사
Married 결혼한
Message 메시지

Novel 소설
Nickname 별명
Skater 스케이트 타는 사람
Snow 눈
Sound 소리
Sports 스포츠
Strange 이상한
Ten thousand 만
Weekend 주말

Dialogue

MORE VOCABULARY: (VERBS): Study and practice saying the following verbs.

Cook 요리하다
Enjoy 즐기다
Dig (땅을) 파다
Drive 운전하다
Fly 날다
Like 좋아하다
Listen 듣다
Live 살다
Love 사랑하다
Return 돌아오다

Send 보내다
Sleep 자다
Smoke 담배 피다
Snow 눈
Spend (시간, 돈) 쓰다
Start 시작하다
Stay 머무르다
Study 공부하다
Sweep 청소하다
Swim 수영하다

Visit 방문하다
Watch 보다
Wear 입다
Work 일하다

Exercise 1

DIALOGUE. Practice this conversation.
다음 대화를 연습 하세요

A. So tell me about your family.
    B. There are four people in my family: my father, my mother, my sister and myself.
A. Where do your parents live?
    B. They live in Taejeon.
A. What's your father's job/What does your father do?
    B. He's an architect.
A. How about your mother?
    B. She's a housewife.
A. What are their hobbies?
    B. They watch movies and play golf.
A. How about your brother?
    B. He's a student and he lives in Seoul.
A. What does he like to do?
    B. He swims/exercises and plays the piano/plays computer games.
A. And you?
    B. I play soccer and read a lot of novels.
A. Does everyone in your family speak English?
    B. Yes, we speak English because we lived in Vancouver for 6 years.

Present Verbs

GRAMMAR REVIEW: PRESENT VERBS 2. Remember, as you learned on page 34, when we use the words "**he**," "**she**," or "**it**" before a verb, the verb will end with the letter "**s**". Look at the examples below. Make sure you study and understand this. 앞에서 주어가 "he," "she," 또는 "it" 인 경우, 동사 뒤에 보통 "**s**"를 붙인 다는 것을 배웠습니다. 다음 예문들을 보면서 다시 한번 연습 하세요.

I live	I work	I like
You live	You work	You like
He/She/It live**s**	**He/She/It** work**s**	**He/She/It** like**s**
We live	We work	We like
They live	They work	They like

Exercise 2

FILL IN THE BLANKS. Please fill in the blanks with the proper verb form. 동사의 형태에 유의하면서 빈칸을 완성 하세요.

1. They . . . . . *live* . . . . . near Itaewon. (live)
2. She . . . . in Kwangju. (live)
3. I . . . . StarCraft, WarCraft and other computer games. (play)
4. We . . . . in the cafeteria. (eat)
5. Let's go to the movie. It . . . . at 7:30. (start)
6. Lee Yeong-pyo . . . . soccer. (play)
7. My mother . . . . breakfast every morning. (cook)
8. His health is bad because he . . . . too many cigarettes. (smoke)
9. Koreans usually . . . . kimchi and rice every day. (eat)
10. Young-min . . . . on Sunday. (swim)
11. Can you . . . . me an email message? (send)
12. Many movies stars . . . . in Beverly Hills. (live)
13. Rich people . . . . expensive cars. (drive)
14. Some marathon runners . . . . more than 100 km a week. (run)
15. In most Korean cities, it . . . . during the winter. (snow)
16. The car . . . . strange noises. (make)
17. They . . . . their new house. (love)
18. Our dog, Rufus, ... a lot of holes. (dig)
19. Hye-won . . . . her boyfriend. (love)
20. I . . . . a good job. (want)
21. Every time she . . . . shopping, she . . . . too much money. (go/spend)
22. They love to . . . . to Jo Sung-mo. (listen)
23. This MP3 player . . . . great. (sound)
24. In my free time, I like to . . . . movies. (watch)
25. During Chu-seok, many Korean women . . . . a lot of food. (cook)
26. In the winter, he always . . . . his boots. (wear)
27. She . . . . the piano. (play)
28. Pilots . . . . airplanes. (fly)

50

Collocations

Exercise 3

JOSH. Fill in the blanks with the appropriate words from the following list: 빈칸에 알맞은 말을 보기에서 골라, 필요하면 동사 형태를 바꾸어 문장을 완성하세요.

| stay | ~~like~~ | speak | sleep | cook | live | live | go |
| return | is | eat | fi | enjoy | read | visit | study |

Josh is a Canadian. He lives in St. Catherines, Ontario, near Niagara Falls. He (1)........ to Brock University. He (2)......... history. He (3).......... in the dormitory at Brock University. He (4)........... his meals in the dormitory and he (5)......... there too. He (6)...*likes*...to play hockey, baseball and football. He also (7)...*plays*..... all kinds of computer games. His friends (8)......... playing computer games too. His favorite hockey team (9).......... the Toronto Maple Leafs. He (10).......... a lot of history books. On weekends, he (11).......... his parents. They (12).......... in Toronto. He (13)......... with them for the whole weekend. His mother often (14).......... him hamburgers and French fries. Because he is from Quebec, he can (15).......... both French and English. On Monday mornings, Josh (16)........ to St. Catherines.

Exercise 4

COLLOCATIONS. Match the verbs in Column A with the appropriate words in Column B. You can use the vocabulary on page 48-49 to help you. B의 단어와 A의 동사들을 알맞게 연결 하세요. p.48-49에 있는 표현들을 참고 하세요.

COLUMN A		COLUMN B
1. wear	K	A. history
2. live	____	B. a car
3. drive	____	C. an email message
4. smoke	____	D. money
5. vacuum	____	E. the carpet
6. study	____	F. sports
7. spend	____	G. in the dormitory
8. play	____	H. a novel
9. send	____	I. cigarettes
10. eat	____	J. the floor
11. sweep	____	K. a coat
12. read	____	L. a meal

Interview

Exercise 5

INTERVIEW 1. Working in groups, ask each other the following questions:

1. Where do you live?
2. Where do you sleep?

I sleep at home.

3. Where do you study?
4. Which sports do you play?
5. Where do you buy clothes?

I buy clothes at . . . .

6. Which school do you go to?
7. Where do you eat breakfast?
8. Where does your family live?

My . . . .

9. What languages do you speak?
10. Where do Germans usually live?

They usually live in . . . .

11. Where do you work/go to school?

I work in Jechon. (I go to school in Osan.)

12. What kind of food do you cook?
13. What kind of books do you read?
14. Where do most French people live?
15. Which color does your mother like?
16. Which computer games do you play?

(You can say, "I don't play computer games.")

17. Which sport does Michelle Wie play?
18. What do you do <u>on</u> Monday mornings?

On Monday mornings, I . . . .

19. What do you do on Saturday?
20. What does your family do on Sunday?
21. What do you do on Wednesday evening?
22. Which languages does your father speak?

He speaks . . . . and . . . .

23. What kind of food does your mother cook?

She cooks . . . .

24. Which soccer players do Koreans like?
25. Which sport do Brazilians play? *(Soccer)*

Eiffel Tower: by Jswieringa

52

Pronunciation

PRONUNCIATION. With your class, practice saying the following words:

1. Dress shoes (**Dress**-shoos)
2. Figure (**Fih**-gur)
3. Freckles (**Frek**-koze)
4. Fan (Fan)
5. Meters (**Mee**-durz)
6. Million (**Mill**-yin)
7. Museum (Myoo-**zee**-uhm)
8. Parent (**Pair**-rint)
9. Province (**Prah**-vince)
10. Remember (Re-**mem**-ber)
11. Season (**See**-zin)
12. Siblings (**Sib**-lingz)
13. Spouse (Spowss)
14. Square (Skwair)
15. Sunglasses (**Sun**-gla-siz)
16. Vegetables (**Veg**-tih-boes)

CUMULATIVE REVIEW. Practice the following review questions with your classmates.

1. Are you married?
2. Is Leonardo DiCaprio handsome?
3. How old are you?
4. Where does Kim Jong-Ill live?
5. Is Ono a good speed skater?
6. What do you do?
7. Is Boa married?
8. Do you have any friends in Daegu?
9. What are you doing?
10. Where do you live?
11. Is China a big country?
12. Do you have a driver's license?
13. Do you have any nicknames?

Unit 6: Have

- **VOCABULARY:** Study the following words.

Beach 해변
Collect stamps 우표 수집하다
Dictionary 사전
Died 죽었다
Digital camera 디지털 카메라
Dress shoes 정장 구두
Equator 적도
Figure 모습
Freckles 주근깨
Grandparents 조부모
Island 섬
Health problem 건강문제
Hobbies 취미
Fan 선풍기
Foreign 외국의
Grandchildren 손자손녀
Important 중요한
Million 백만
Museum 박물관
Nuclear weapons 핵무기
Month 달
Own (verb) 소유하다

Parent 부(모)
Pet 애완동물
Pocket 주머니
Province 지방
Remember 기억하다
Shark 상어
Season 계절
Siblings 형제자매
Side 면
Snake 뱀
Spouse 배우자
Square 네모
State (In the USA) 주
Sunglasses 선글라스
Team 팀
Triangle 삼각형
TV station 방송국
Vegetables 야채
Weapon 무기
Week 주
Year 해
Zero 0 (영)

Dialogue

Exercise

DIALOGUE. With your class and possibly in groups, practice this conversation. Please refer to this dialogue to assist you with future exercises in this unit.
다음 대화를 연습하고, 연습 문제를 공부할 때 참고 하세요.

A. Do you have any brothers?
    B. Yes, I have many brothers.
A. How many brothers do you have?
    B. I have four brothers.
A. Wow! How many sisters do you have?
    B. I have one sister.
A. So, you have five siblings.
    B. That's right.
A. Do you have any grandparents?
    B. No, I don't have any grandparents. They all died.
A. I'm sorry to hear that.
    B. That's okay. They died when I was very young. I don't remember them.

GRAMMAR 1: HAVE. The verb "have" is often used in the English language. Study the following examples of how we use this verb. 다음 예문을 보면서 동사 "have" 를 연습 하세요.

I have	For example: I **have** a sister
You have	For example: You **have** a nice car
He has	For example: He **has** many friends
She has	For example: She **has** a nice figure
It has	For example: It **has** five bedrooms
We have	For example: We **have** lots of food
They have	For example: They **have** no money

GRAMMAR 2: DON'T HAVE. Study more examples of how we use have.

I don't have	For example: I **don't have** an iPod
You don't have	For example: You **don't have** a fast car
He doesn't have	For example: He <u>**doesn't** have</u> much money
She doesn't have	For example: She <u>**doesn't** have</u> a boyfriend
It doesn't have	For example: It <u>**doesn't** have</u> a swimming pool
We don't have	For example: We **don't have** enough water
They don't have	For example: They **don't have** your computer

Have

HAVE. For each of the following, fill in the blanks with **have** or **has**. "have" 또는 "has"를 넣어 빈칸을 완성 하세요.

1. I only ....*have*...... one computer.
2. They ...... too many health problems.
3. Tiger Woods ...... a Swedish wife.
4. She .... no children.
5. A car .... four wheels.
6. They .... many vegetables.
7. We .... three parties.
8. Home Plus ...... too many customers.
9. South Korea ...... 48,000,000 people.
10. You .... two cars.
11. We .... ten more minutes.
12. This novel .... 300 pages.

DON'T HAVE/DOESN'T HAVE. For each of the following fill in the blanks with **don't have** or **doesn't have**.

1. I ... *don't have*... a computer.
2. They .... any friends.
3. She .... any money.
4. Ju-hee .... a snowboard.
5. Many Africans .... enough food.
6. My wife .... a car.
7. Our city .... a big hotel.
8. Singapore .... snow.
9. This park .... a zoo.
10. Elephants.................... any hair.
11. My son .... have a girlfriend.
12. Ji-sun.................... an iPod.

Interview

Exercise 4

INTERVIEW 1: DO YOU HAVE? As usual, interview your classmates. Remember, try not to read as you listen to the questions.
친구들에게 인터뷰 하세요. 질문을 들을 때는 책을 보지 마세요.

1. Do you have a cell phone?
    A. *Yes, I have a cell phone.*
2. Do you have many friends?
    A. *Yes, I have many friends.*
    A. *No, I don't have many friends.*
3. Do you have a lot of homework?
    A. *Yes, I have a lot of homework.*
    A. *No, I don't have a lot of homework.*
4. Does Tom Cruise have a wife?
    A. *Yes, Tom has a wife.*
    A. *Yes, he has a wife.*
5. Do you have a cell phone?
6. Do you have a sister?
    A. *No, I don't have a sister.*
7. Do you have a computer?
8. Do you have an electronic dictionary?
9. . . . . . . .have a cat?
10. . . . . . . .have a husband/wife?
11. . . . . a digital camera?
12. . . . . a watch?
13. . . . . lots of clothes?
No, I don't have a lot of . . . . .
14. Does your sister/brother have a job?
(*I don't have a brother.*)
15. Does Bill Gates have a lot of money?
16. . . . . Seoul have many people?
17. . . . . .Seoul have a beach?
18. Does Daegu have a subway?
19. Do your parents have a computer?
20. Does your computer have Internet?
21. Does Roh Moo-hyun have an important job?
22. . . . . . . Sim Eun-ha have a husband?
23. Do elephants have hair?
24. What are 10 things that you have?

Cell Phone Pocket: by Misocrazy

Grammar

GRAMMAR 3: ANY. If someone asks "*Do you have any...?*" your answer can be "*No, I don't have any...*" or

> Yes, I have a . . .
> Yes, I have one…
> Yes, I have two…
> Yes, I have some. . .
> Yes, I have many . . .
>
> **REMEMBER THIS:** no → any   yes → some/a/one/two/many
>
> EXAMPLE:
>
> NO
> Q: Do you have any apples?
>   A: **No**, I don't have **any** apples.
> YES
> Q: Do you have any apples?
>   A: **Yes**, I have **some** apples.

1. Do you have any grandparents?
     Yes, I have a grandmother.
     No, I don't have any grandparents.
2. Do you have any pets?
     Yes, I have two cats.
     No, I don't have any pets.
3. Do you have any money?
     Yes, I have 10,000 won.
     Yes, I have some money.
     No, I don't have any money.
4. Do you have any water?
     Yes, I have some water.
     No, I don't have any water.
5. Do you have any friends in Daegu?
     Yes, I have many friends in Daegu.
     Yes, I have some friends in Daegu.
     No, I don't have any friends in Daegu.
6. Does Gina have any books?
     Yes, she has four books.
     No, she doesn't have any books.
7. Does South Korea have any nuclear weapons? *I don't know if South Korea has any nuclear weapons.*

Interview

Exercise 5

MULTIPLE CHOICE. For each of the following, choose the best answer. 다음 중 정답을 고르세요.

1. Do you have ...... oranges?
a. a   b. any
2. **No**, I don't have .... oranges.
a. some   b. any
3. Do you have .... water?
a. a   b. any
4. Yes, I have .... water.
a. some   b. many
5. Do you have .... freckles?
a. a   b. any
6. **No**, I don't have .... freckles.
a. any   b. some
7. Yes, I have .... freckles
a. any   b. some.
8. Yes, I have .... freckles.
a. any   b. many
9. Does Seoul have .... museums?
a. a   b. any
10. Yes, Seoul has .... museums.
a. any   b. about forty
11. Do they have .... juice?
a. any   b. a
12. **No**, they don't have .... juice.
a. any   b. some

Exercise 6

INTERVIEW 2: DO YOU HAVE ANY…? Interview your classmates. Look at *Grammar 3* for assistance.
다음 문장들을 친구들에게 인터뷰 하세요. Grammar 3를 참고하세요.

1. Do you have <u>any</u> grandchildren?
   <u>No</u>, I don't have <u>any</u> grandchildren.
2. Do you have <u>any</u> vegetables?
   <u>Yes</u>, I have <u>some</u> vegetables.
3. Do you have any brothers?
   <u>Yes</u>, I have <u>one</u> brother.
4. Do you have any sisters?
   <u>Yes</u>, I have <u>three</u> sisters.
5. Do you have any aunts?
6. ..... you have any dress shoes?
7. ..... have any sunglasses?
8. ..... any hobbies?
9. ..... any money?
10. ..... any foreign friends?
11. ..... any friends in Sokch'o?
12. ..... any friends in Canada?
13. ..... any DVDs?
14. Does South Korea have any islands?
    <u>Yes</u>, it has <u>some</u> islands.
15. Do you have any freckles?
16. Does Boa have any children?
17. Do we have any English classes next week?
18. Does South Korea have any mountains?
19. Does Tom Cruise have any children? (yes)
20. Does Australia have any beaches?
21. Does Pusan have any beaches?
22. Does your mother have any health problems?
23. Does Bill Gates have any money?

How Many?

GRAMMAR 4: HOW MANY? Study the following examples. If someone has **more than one** (1) unit (for example, more than "one apple"), there is usually an "s" added to the end of the noun (for example, **two** apple**s**). Also, we say "**No** apple**s**." 한 개 이상을 의미할 때 명사 뒤에 "s"를 붙입니다.
If there is only **one** unit (for example, one apple or an apple), then you don't need to add an "s" to the end of the noun (apple).

One brother	She has **one** uncle
Two brother**s**	Tom Cruise has many fan**s**
One car	Canada has four season**s**
Three car**s**	They have no computer**s**
One week	They have **a** computer
Five week**s**	He has **one** car
A friend	It has no leg**s**
Many friend**s**	South Korea has many mountain**s**
A city	We have many friend**s**
Some citie**s**	He doesn't have **a** girlfriend
I have four brother**s**	Seoul has 12 universitie**s**
I have **one** sister	The Earth has **one** equator

Exercise 7

FILL IN THE BLANKS. For each of the following, fill in the blanks with the proper form of the noun. 명사의 형태에 유의하면서 빈칸을 완성 하세요.

1. I have three . . .*cars* . . . . (car)
2. She has one . . . . (TV)
3. I have one . . . . (dog)
4. He has no . . . . (friend)
5. We have three . . . . (dog)
6. I have many . . . . (car)
7. They have eight . . . . (color)
8. I don't have a . . . . (car)
9. We have no . . . . (student)
10. You have one . . . . (computer)
11. They have many . . . . (computer)
12. I have one . . . . (brother)
13. It has some . . . . (tree)
14. Hye-min has two . . . . (boyfriend)

How Many?

Exercise 8

HOW MANY? Ask each other the following questions.

1. How many wheels does it have? *It has two wheels.*	2. How many dogs does he have?
3. How many boxes does he have?	4. How many children do they have?
5. How many legs does he have?	6. How many countries does it have?
7. How many colors do they have?	8. How many books does she have?
9. How many trees does it have?	10. How many windows does it have?

Interview

INTERVIEW 3. Interview one another by asking the following questions.
다음 문장들을 서로 인터뷰 하세요.

1. How many cars do you have?
I have no cars.
I don't have any cars.
2. How many teeth does your baby have?
My baby/He/She has two teeth.
3. How many provinces does Canada have?
Canada/It has ten provinces.
4. How many houses do you own?
I don't own any houses.
5. How many cars do you own?
I own one car.
6. How many teeth do sharks have?
Sharks/They have many teeth.
7. How many fingers do you have?
I have . . . . . . fingers.
8. How many friends do you have?
9. How many brothers do you have?
10. How many legs does a horse have?
A horse has . . . . . . legs.
It has . . . . . . legs.
11. How many cities does China have? (many)
12. How many legs does a snake have?
13. How many days does a week have?
14. How many computers do you have?
15. How many cell phones do you have?
16. How many sides does a square have?
17. How many months does a year have?
18. How many minutes does an hour have? (60)
19. How many colors does a rainbow have? (7)
20. How many universities does Seoul have? (12)
21. How many meters does a kilometer have? (1,000)
22. How many provinces does South Korea have? (7)
23. How many states does the United States have? (50)

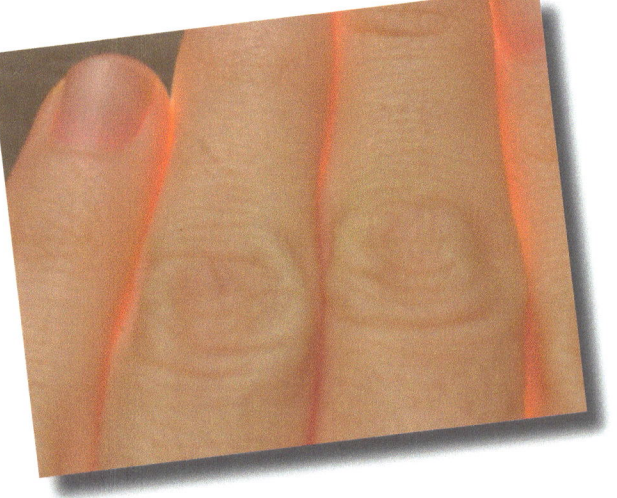

Fingers: by gshowman

Pronunciation

PRONUNCIATION TIP: THOUSAND: Don't forget, the word "and" usually sounds like "**in**." The number **247,893** almost sounds like "***two-hundred-in for-dee seven thowsind, eight-hundrid-in nigh-nee-three.***"

Exercise 10

NUMBERS. (Continued from page 27) Now practice saying the following:

1. 370 (*Three hundred in sevenee-three*)
2. 692
3. 770
4. 5387. 9,000
8. 9,060
9. 9,600
10. 19,600
11. 19,690
12. 119,690
13. 119,619
14. 190,119
15. 519,590
16. 683,143
17. 983,465
18. 247,893
19. 450,187
20. 800,003
21. 852,203
22. 173,400
23. 117,657
24. 170,021

Exercise 11

ACCENT REDUCTION. With your class, practice pronouncing these:

1. Amusement park (*A-**myooz**-mint park*)
2. Athlete (***Ath**-leet*)
3. Caribbean (***Kair**-ri-be-in*) or (*kur-**ri**-be-in*)
4. Computer (*Com-**pyoo**-der*)
5. Draught beer (***draft**-beer*)
6. Freckles (***Freck**-koes*)
7. Friends (***Frenz***)
8. Hot and spicy (***Hawt**-in spigh-see*)
9. Hour (***Ow**-wer*)
10. Many (***Men**-nee*)
11. Minute (***Min**-nit*)
12. Phone (*fone*) or (*foan*)
13. Season (***See**-zin*)
14. Water (***Wah**-der*)
15. Wheel (*Wea*l or *Weel*)

Countries

COUNTRIES. With your class, practice pronouncing the following:

1. Australia (*Aus-**tray**-lee-ah*)
2. Brazil (*Brih-**zil***)
3. Canada (***Can**'a-da*)
4. Great Britain (***Brih**-tin*)
5. England (***Eng**-glind*)
6. Finland (***Finn**-lind*)
7. Poland (***Poe**-lind*)
8. New Zealand (*New-**Zee**-lind*)
9. Switzerland (***Switz**-zer-lind*)
10. Scotland (***Scott**-lind*)
11. France (*Franss*)
12. Germany (***Ger**-min-Ee*)
13. Korea (*Kor-**ree**-ah*)
14. Iraq (*I-**rack***)
15. Russia (***Ruh**-Shuh*)
16. Sweden (***Swee**-din*)
17. Singapore (***Sing**-ga-poar*)
18. South Africa (*South **Aff**-ri-ka*)
19. Jamaica (*Ja-**may**-ka*)
20. Thailand (***Tie**-land*)
21. United States (*The **U**-nigh-did States*)

CUMULATIVE REVIEW. With your class and in groups, practice the following review questions:
다음 문장들을 다시 한번 연습 하세요.

1. How do you spell your first name?
2. Are you comfortable?
3. Is Tony Blair French? *(No)*
4. Is today snowy?
5. Do you eat kim-pap?
6. Does Pardeep study English?
7. Do you have an MP3 player?
8. Does Gus Hidink have a good job?
9. Do you have any freckles?
10. Does Yong-in have any amusement parks?
11. How many sides does a triangle have?
12. Where do you eat lunch?
13. Which language do French people speak?
14. Which sport does Tiger Woods play?
15. Do you have many friends in this class?
16. Do you have a dog?

Unit 7: Hobbies, Likes and Dislikes

• **VOCABULARY**: Study these words and then practice saying them with your class.

Action movies 액션영화
Amusement park 놀이공원
Athlete 운동선수
Beach 해변
The best 최고
Carrot 당근
Chess 체스
Coconut soup 코코넛 수프
Draught beer (*draft beer*) 생맥주
Favorite 가장 좋아하는
Free time 여가시간
Hobby 취미
Horror movies 공포영화
Intelligent 똑똑한
"It's so-so" 그저그래
"Oh my God!" 오, 저런!
Romantic comedies 로맨틱 코미디
Season 계절
Spicy food 매운 음식
Summer 여름
Taking care of children 아이들을 돌보다
Tennis 테니스
Thai food 타이 음식
TV drama 드라마
War 전쟁
Weather 날씨
Wine 와인
Winter 겨울
"What kind of…" 어떤 종류…
"What type of…" 어떤 타입…

Dialogue

MORE VOCABULARY (VERBS):

Can't stand 참을 수 없다
Crazy about ~에 대해 열광하다
Cycling 사이클링
Dance 춤추다
Dislike 싫어하다
Do taekwondo 태권도하다
Doing dishes 설거지하다
Exercising 운동하는
Hate 미워하다
Lift weights 역기
Love 사랑하다
Play the guitar 기타 연주하다
Play the piano 피아노 치다
Prefer 선호하다
Spend money 돈을 쓰다
Surf the Internet 인터넷 하다
Weight lifting 역기
Weight training 웨이트 트레이닝
White water rafting 레프팅하다
Writing exams 쓰기 시험
"You'd better…"
당신은 하는 편이 낫다…

Exercise 1

DIALOGUE 1. Practice the following conversation with your classmates.

Dong-gu: What are your hobbies?

Mi-hee: My hobbies are cooking, shopping and listening to music.

Mi-hee: What is your hobby?

Dong-gu: My hobby is watching TV.

Dong-gu: How about you Jay-Won? What do you do in your free time?

Jay-won: In my free time, I like to travel, play soccer and go to Caribbean Bay.

Jay-won: How about you and your girlfriend, what do you like to do?

Dong-gu: I like to watch TV. My girlfriend likes to swim, play the piano and watch movies.

Mi-hee: What is your girlfriend's hobby?

Jay-won: Her hobby is snowboarding.

Mi-hee: How about shopping?

Jay-won: Oh yeah, she loves to go shopping too.

Dong-gu: I think most girls love shopping.

Mi-hee and Jay-Won: Yes, and spending money.

Collocations

Exercise 2

COLLOCATIONS. Match the verbs in Column A with the appropriate nouns in Column B.

COLUMN A		COLUMN B
1. Play	_____	A. StarCraft
2. Watch	_____	B. the Internet
3. Drink	_____	C. the dishes
4. Climb	_____	D. stamps
5. Play	__G__	E. man-du
6. Do	_____	F. TV
7. Eat	_____	G. chess
8. Surf	_____	H. to music
9. Take care of	_____	I. mountains
10. Collect	_____	J. weights
11. Listen	_____	K. children
12. Lift	_____	L. Mak-geol-li

GRAMMAR 1: DOES NOT . . . . Look at the following examples.

CORRECT EXAMPLES
1. He does not like ✓
2. She does not like ✓
3. It does not like ✓
4. She does not play ✓
5. He does not eat ✓

INCORRECT EXAMPLES
1. She does not like<u>s</u> ✗
2. He does not like<u>s</u> ✗
3. It does not like<u>s</u> ✗
4. She does not play<u>s</u> ✗
5. He does not eat<u>s</u> ✗

67

Hobbies

Exercise 3

INTERVIEW 1: HOBBIES. Interview your classmates. Use the *Hobbies* table to help answer the questions. Use this pattern to answer them: "**His hobbies are a-*ing*, b-*ing*, c-*ing* and d-*ing*.**" 다음을 친구들에게 인터뷰 하세요. 위의 표 *Hobbies*를 참고하고, "His hobbies are a-*ing*, b-*ing*, c-*ing* and d-*ing*." 와 같은 문장으로 대답 하세요.

HOBBIES

Name	First Hobby	Second Hobby	Third Hobby
Dong-gu	watching TV		
Mi-hee	cooking	shopping	listening to music
Jay-won	travel	play soccer	going to Caribbean Bay
Dong-gu's girlfriend	swim	play the piano	watch movies
Jay-won's girlfriend	snowboarding	shopping	

1. What <u>are</u> your brother's hobbies?

<u>His</u> hobbies <u>are</u> fishing, hiking <u>and</u> snowboarding.

2. What <u>is</u> your father's hobby?

<u>His</u> hobby <u>is</u> mountain climbing.

3. What are your hobbies?

4. . . . . are Dong-gu's girlfriend's hobbies?

5. . . . . Mi-hee's hobbies?

6. . . . . Dong-gu's hobby?

7. . . . . Jay-won's hobbies?

8. . . . . Jay-won's girlfriend's hobbies?

9. Does Mi-hee like watching TV?

No, she doesn't like watching TV.

10. . . . . . . Dong-gu like watching TV?

11. . . . . . . Jay-won like going to Caribbean Bay?

12. . . . . . Jay-won like playing baseball?

Baseball: by Gniliep

Interview

Exercise 4

INTERVIEW 2: "LIKE TO..." Interview your classmates. Use the *Hobbies* and this pattern: "**He likes to a, b, c and d**." 다음을 친구들에게 인터뷰 하세요. 위의 표 *Hobbies*를 참고하고, "He likes to a, b, c and d." 와 같은 문장으로 대답 하세요.

1. What does your brother <u>like to</u> do? *He <u>likes to</u> fish, hike <u>and</u> climb mountains.*

2. What does your father <u>like to</u> do in his free time? *He <u>likes to</u> climb mountains.*

3. What does your mother do in her free time?

4. What do you like to do in your free time?

5. . . . . Dong-gu like to do in his free time?

6. . . . . Jay-won like to do?

7. . . . . Jay-won's girlfriend like to do?

8. . . . . Dong-gu's girlfriend like to do?

9. . . . . Mi-hee like to do in her free time?

10. Does Mi-hee like to snowboard?

11. . . . . Dong-gu like to swim in his free time?

12. . . . . Jay-won like to travel?

13. . . . . . . Jay-won like to play hockey?

Hockey: by Tknoxb

Hobbies

Exercise

HOBBIES. Develop questions and then ask your classmates.

EXAMPLES:
1. A. What is her hobby?
   B. *Her hobby is listening to music.*
   Or A. What does she like to do?
   B. *She likes to listen to music.*

2. A. What is their hobby?
   B. *Their hobby is cycling.*
   Or A. What do they like to do?
   B. *They like to ride their bicycles.*

1. 2.  3.  4. 
5.  6.  7.  8. 
9.  10.  11.  12. 
13.  14.  15.  16.

Answers for Exercise 5.
1. Her hobby is listening to music.
2. His hobby is cycling.
3. His hobby is playing chess.
4. Her hobby is weight training.
5. His hobby is playing tennis.
6. Her hobby is watching TV.
7. Her hobby is dancing.
8. Their hobby is playing the guitar.
9. Her hobby is swimming.
10. Their hobby is traveling.
11. Her hobby is cooking.
12. His hobby is playing the piano.
13. Their hobby is whitewater rafting.
14. He likes to play chess.
15. They like to play hockey.
16. Their hobby is taek-won-do.
1. She likes to listen to music.
2. They like to ride their bicycles.
3. He likes to play chess.
4. She likes to lift weights.
5. He likes to play tennis.
6. She likes to watch TV.
7. She likes to dance.
8. They like to do taek-won-do.
9. She likes to swim.
10. They like to travel.
11. She likes to cook.
12. He likes to play the piano.
13. They like to go whitewater rafting.
14. He likes fishing.
15. They like to play hockey.
16. She likes to play the guitar.

Dialogue

Exercise 6

DIALOGUE 2. With your class and then in groups, practice the following dialogue. Students should be able to repeat the conversation without looking at it (Some memorizing will be necessary). 대화를 연습하고 문장을 외울 수 있도록 반복 연습 하세요.

A: Do you like movies?
    B: Yes, I like movies.
A: What kind of movies do you like?
    B: I like action movies/romantic comedies/horror movies.
A: Who's your favorite movie star?
    B: My favorite movie star is Bruce Willis.
A: Bruce Willis! I love/I'm crazy about/I really like Bruce Willis! He's my favorite movie star too.
    B: Yeah, he's the best!

Exercise 7

HOW MUCH DO YOU LIKE IT? Label the following with **crazy about, like, so-so, dislike,** and **can't stand.**

How much do you like it?

| *****Love (Crazy about) |
| ****Like |
| *** It's okay (It's so-so) |
| **Dislike (don't like) |
| *Hate (Can't stand) |

1. _____ 2. _____ 3. _____ 4. _____ 5. _____

What Do You Think Of ...?

Exercise 8

INTERVIEW 3: WHAT DO YOU THINK OF . . . ? Ask your classmates the following questions. Use expressions such as **"love"**, **"crazy about"**, **"like"**, **"dislike"**, **"don't like"**, **"hate"**, **"okay"**, **"so so"** and **"can't stand"**. 다음을 연습하면서 "love", "crazy about", "like", "dislike", "don't like", "hate", "okay", "so so" and "can't stand" 와 같은 다양한 표현을 이용해 대답 하세요.

1. **Do you like** soccer? *Yes, I like soccer.*
2. Do you like music? *No, I don't like music.*
3. Do you like shopping?
Yes, I love shopping.
4. **What do you think of** George Bush?
I hate George Bush. (He's so so)
5. Do you like Japanese food?
No, I can't stand Japanese food.
6. What do you think of horror movies?
They're okay.
7. Do you like spicy food?
8. What do you think of classical music?
9. What do you think of Rain (Bi)?
10. . . . . today's weather?
11. . . . . strawberry ice cream?
12. . . . . Lotteria?
13 Do you like Park Sin-yang?
14. . . . . like comic books?
15. . . . . like rainy days?
16. . . . . your hometown?
17. . . . . doing the dishes?
18 . . . . surfing the Internet?
19. . . . . of Lee Myung-bak?
20. . . . . taking care of children?
21. . . . . watching American TV dramas?
22. . . . . mountain climbing?
23. . . . . soju?
24. . . . . naeng-myeon?
25. . . . . writing exams?
26. . . . . of your family?
27. . . . . of this English class?
28. . . . . of Americans?
29. . . . . Korean food?
30. . . . . of Tom Hanks?
31. . . . . Johnny Depp?
32. . . . . Big Mamma?

Yo Sushi: by PMorgan

Interview

Exercise 9

INTERVIEW 4: WHAT IS YOUR FAVORITE?

1. What <u>is</u> your favorite movie?
My favorite movie is J.S.A.
2. What's your favorite food?
3. .... favorite color?
4. .... animal?
5. .... city?
6. .... sport?
7. .... book?
8. .... ice cream?
9. .... drink?
10. .... song?
11. Who is your favorite athlete?
12. Who is your favorite movie star?
13. .... favorite singer?
14. .... writer?
15. .... English teacher?

Exercise 10

MI-HEE. With your class, ask and answer the following questions. Then in groups, you can ask your classmates what kind of beer, pizza, soda etc. they like. Remember, **"What type of"** = **"What kind of"**.

1. What kind of beer does Mi-hee like?
She likes draught beer.
2. What type of food does Mi-hee like?
3. What kind of soda .... ?
4. What type of .... ?
5. What ...... juice .... ?
6. What .... ?
7. .... wine .... ?
8. .... vegetable**s** .... ?

MI-HEE'S LIKES

Dialogue

Exercise 11

DIALOGUE 3. WHAT KIND OF? Again, with your class and then with your classmates (in groups), practice the following conversation.

A. What kind of food do you like?
    B. I like Korean food and Thai food.
A. Korean food! I hate/I can't stand Korean food! It's too hot and spicy.
    B. Really! I love it/I'm crazy about it.
A. What's Thai food like?
    B. Thai food is like Korean food: very hot and spicy.
A. Oh my God! I don't want to eat Thai food.
    B. No, you'd better not.
A. What do you prefer, Thai food or Korean food?
    B. I prefer Thai food because I love coconut soup.

Exercise 12

INTERVIEW 5. Again, interview your classmates.

1. What kind of food do you like? *I like spicy food*.
2. What type of men/woman do you like? *I like intelligent/good looking men/women.*
3. What do you prefer, kimchi-jigae or dwenjang-jigae? *I prefer kimchi-jigae.*
4. What kind of sports do you like? *I like soccer, baseball and taekwondo.*
5. What kind of sports do you dislike?
6. What type of music do you like?
7. What kind of ice cream do you like?
8. . . . . food do you like?
9. . . . . you dislike? *I dislike Mexican food.*
10. . . . . movies do you like?
11. What type of movies do you dislike?
12. What do you prefer, pizza or hamburger?
13. What do you prefer, mountains or beaches?
14. . . . ., Hite or Cass?
15. . . . . , romantic comedies or action movies?
16. . . . . , Korean movies or American movies?
17. Which actress do you prefer, Kim Hee-sun, or Choi Ji-woo?
18. . . . ., Tom Cruise or Brad Pitt?
19. Which music do you prefer, Korean or American?
20. . . . ., Seoul or Pusan?
21. . . . ., winter or summer?

Nationalities

Exercise 13

REWRITING. Rewrite the following questions and answers.

1. hobby is your what? . . . . *What is your hobby?* . . . .
2. Internet my the is hobby surfing . . . . . . *My hobby is surfing the Internet.* . . . .
3. to do does like Mi-hee what? . . . .
4. Mi-hee likes to music listen to . . . .
5. what like kind of you movies do?. . . . .
6. I comedies like . . . .
7. what sport favorite your is? . . . .
8. favorite basketball sport is my . . . .

Exercise 14

PRONUNCIATION: NATIONALITIES. With your class, practice pronouncing the following words.

1. Australian (*Auss-**tray**-lee-yin*)
2. Brazilian (*Brah-**zil**-yin*)
3. Canadian (*Kin-**ay**-dee-yin*)
4. Korean (*Kor-**ree**-yin*)
5. Singaporean (*Sing-ga-**poar**-ree-yin*)
6. British (***Bri**-dish*)
7. Swedish (***Swee**-dish*)
8. English (***Eng**-glish*)
9. Finnish (***Fin**-nish*)
10. Polish (***Poe**-lish*)
11. French (*French*)
12. Jamaican (*Ja-**may**-kin*)
13. American (*A-**mair**-rih-kin*)
14. South African (*Sowth **Aff**-rih-kin*)
15. German (***Ger**-min*)
16. Russian (***Ruh**-shin*)
17. Iraqi (*I-**ra'**key*)
18. New Zealander (*New-**zee**-lin-der*)
19. Swiss (*Swiss*)
20. Thai (*Tie*)

Korean Flag: by Arkansas Lad

Pronunciation

Exercise 15

PRONUNCIATION.

1. Busy (*Biz-zee*)
2. Climb (*clime*)
3. Enough (*Ee-nuff*)
4. Flu (*Floo or Flew*)
5. Hate (*Hait*)
6. Headache (*Hed'aik*)
7. Idea (*I-D-ah*)
8. Pizza (*Peet—za*)
9. Sauna (*Saw-nah*)
10. Sure (*Sher*) (Same sounds as "her")
11. Toothache (*Too-thaik*)
12. What are you going to do? (*Wuh-dar-u-goo-na-doo?*)
13. What do you want to do? (*Wuh-doo-u-Wan-na-doo?*)

Exercise 16

CUMULATIVE REVIEW.

1. What is your favorite TV show?
2. What are your hobbies?
3. Do you like your hair-style?
4. What is your e-mail address?
5. Is your English teacher married?
6. What do you prefer, juice or cola?
7. What do you do?
8. What do you do in your free time?
9. Are Won Bin and Park Ji-sung Japanese?
10. Do you like Ahn Jang-hwan?
11. Are you from China?
12. Where is Celine Dion from?
13. What type of books do you like?
14. How old is Kim Dae-jung?

Unit 8: Let's Go Out

• **VOCABULARY:** Study these words and phrases and then practice saying them with your class.

"Are you *free* tonight?" 오늘 밤에 시간 되세요?
Boring 지루한
Busy 바쁜
Clean 깨끗한
A cold 감기
The flu 독감
Have to ~ 해야만 한다
Headache 독감
"I have a cold" 감기에 걸렸어요
"I have the flu" 독감에 걸렸어요
"I'd love to" ~ 하고 싶다
"Let's . . . ?" ~ 하자
Meet 만나다
Sick 아픈
Sure 물론이지
"That sounds great!" 좋아요!
Tired 피곤한
Toothache 치통
"That sounds like fun" 재미있겠다!
"We should . . ." 우리는 ~ 해야만 한다
"What are you going to do?" 뭐 할꺼예요?
"What do you want to do"? 뭐하고 싶으세요?

"What should we do?" 뭘 해야 하지요?
"Why don't we . . . ?" 우리 ~ 할까요?

77

Expressions

MORE VOCABULARY (VERBS):

"go for a bike ride" 자전거 타러 가다
"go for a drink" 술한잔 하러 가다
"go for pizza" 피자 먹으러 가다
Have to ~ 해야만 한다
Should ~ 해야만 한다
"We should..." 우리는 ~ 해야만 한다

COMMON QUESTIONS:
What should we do?
What do you want to do?

COMMON SUGGESTIONS:
"Let's watch TV!" = "Why don't we watch TV!" = "We should watch TV!"

COMMON RESPONSES:
Yes = Sure = Okay

Exercise 1

EXPRESSIONS. With your class, practice saying the following:

1. What should we do? What do you want to do?

Let's . . . Why don't we . . . We should . . .	…stay home and watch TV …go to a PC Room …go to a DVD room …go to a movie …go to a soccer game …go to a sauna …play video games …play StarCraft …play baseball …play cards …watch TV …listen to some music …surf the Internet …go for dinner …go for a swim …go for a walk …go for a drink …go for a coffee …go for a beer …go for a bike ride …go for a drive …go for a run …go swimming …go snowboarding …go fishing …go shopping …go hiking …go mountain climbing …go golfing …go dancing …go for pizza …have dinner

2. YES

Yes, . . . Sure, . . . Okay, . . .	…that sounds great …that sounds like a good idea …that sounds like fun …I'd love to …good idea

3. NO

No, . . . No, I can't . . . I'm sorry, . . .	…I don't have any money …I don't have enough money …I don't have any time …I'm busy …I'm too busy …I'm sick …I have a cold/the flu… …I have a headache/toothache… …I'm too tired …we went there yesterday …we did that yesterday …that's too boring …I have to study …I have to meet my friend …I have to work …I have to clean the house …I have to cook dinner

MORE EXPRESSIONS:
Have to = must
What are you going to do?
What are you going to do tonight?
Are you free tonight? = Do you have free time tonight?
Are you free Friday night? *(Free = not busy)*

Dialogue

Exercise 2

DIALOGUE. Practice the following interview with your classmates. (Students should be able to perform this dialogue without reading it. Some memorizing will be required.) 다음 대화를 연습 하세요. 지문을 안 보고 대화 할 수 있도록 연습 하세요.

A: What do you want to do tonight?
    B: Let's go to a PC room.
A: No, we did that yesterday.
    B: Why don't we go swimming?
A: No, I'm too tired.
    B: Why don't we go to a night club?
A: I'm sorry, I hate night clubs.
    B: We should go to a movie.
A: I can't. I don't have enough money.
    B: Then, let's stay home and study English.
A: Okay, that sounds great!

Exercise 3

MATCHING. Complete the following conversation by matching Column A with Column B. A와 B를 연결하여 대화를 완성하세요..

COLUMN A	COLUMN B
1. What should ____	A. we do?
2. Why don't ____	B. sounds great!
3. I'm sorry. I don't have ____	C. for a bike ride.
4. Let's go ____	D. stay home and watch a DVD.
5. I can't ____	E. I'm too tired.
6. Then let's ____	F. we go to a movie?
7. Okay, that ____	G. any money.

Let's Go To The Park

Exercise 4

MATCHING 2. Do the same thing as in Exercise 3.
Exercise 3과 같이 대화를 연습하세요.

COLUMN A	COLUMN B
1A. What should . B .	A. don't we go to a movie?
1B. Why . . .	B. we do?
1A No. we don't have any . . .	C. cards?
1B Let's stay	D. want to do?
1A Sure, I'd . . .	E. to go see a doctor.
2A. What do you . . .	F. home and watch TV.
2B. Why don't we go to a PC . . .	G. money.
2A. No. . . .	H. surf the Internet.
2B. Let's listen . . .	I. Room?
2A. I'm sorry. I have . . .	J. a good idea.
3A. Why don't we play . . .	K. to some music.
3B. Yes, that sounds . . .	L. movie someday.
4A. Let's . . .	M. love to.
4B. I'm . . .	N. going to do?
5A. What are you . . .	O. I can't. I'm very sick.
5B. I have to . . .	P. great!
5A. And then, I have to clean . . .	Q. work.
5B. Let's go to a . . .	R. the house.
5A. Sure. That sounds like . . .	S. sorry. I have to work.

Exercise 5

LET'S. With a partner make suggestions using "**Let's**…". If the answer is no, give a reason. (You can also look for "no" reasons at the beginning of this unit.) 파트너에게 "Lets…" 구문을 이용해 다음을 질문 하세요. "no"인 경우에는 그림을 잘 보고 그 이유를 말하세요.

1.

A. <u>Let's go to the park.</u>　　　　B. <u>I'm sorry, I'm sick</u>

80

Let's

2.

A. *Let's go dancing* .   B. *Sure. That sounds great!*

3

A. _____   B. _____

4.

A. _____   B. _____*Okay, good idea.*_____

5.

A. _____   B. _____

6.

A. _____   B. _____

Let's

1.

A. _Let's go to the park._   B. _I'm sorry, I'm sick_

2.

A. _Let's go dancing_   .   B. _Sure. That sounds great!_

3

A. _____   B. _Okay, good idea._

4.

A. _____   B. _____

5.

A. _____   B. _____

6.

Conversation

Exercise 6 — REWRITE the following conversations.

CONVERSATION 1

1. A: are going do to you what? .... *What are you going to do?* ....

2. B: movie to a let's go ....

3. A: I don't I'm have money enough sorry ....

4. B: let's swimming go ....

5. A: sorry I'm too I'm tired ....

6. B: we play should StarCraft. ....

7. A: good idea Okay ....

CONVERSATION 2

8. A: should do we what? ....

9. B: go let's shopping ....

10. A: any money I have I don't can't ....

11. B: to go why we don't COEX? ....

12. A: idea that's great a yes ....

CONVERSATION 3

1. A: watch TV let's ....

2. B: No, boring that's ....

3. C: I'm I'm busy sorry. ....

4. D: no, I have work to I can't ....

5. A: Insadong we why don't to go? ....

6. B: to I'd love sure ....

83

Let's Go Out

Exercise 7 — CROSSWORD

Across
1. Let's _____ Starcraft.
4. That _____ great!
5. What _____ you want to do?
6. I have to _____ my friend.
9. Why don't we go for a _____ ride.
15. Why don't we go _____
17. We_____ listen to some music.
18. I'm sorry. I don't have _____ money.
19. Why don't we go for a _____
21. What _____ you going to do?.
22. Let's stay _____ and watch TV.

Down
2. Let's _____ to some music.
3. _____ , I'd love to.
4. Let's go _____
7. I'm going to a PC _____
8. _____ go to a video room.
10. _____ don't we go for a drink?
11. I have to cook _____
12. We should go to a _____
13. That's a great _____ !
14. I'm sorry, I _____ to study.
16. _____ should go for a coffee.
20. I'm sorry. I'm _____ tired.

84 *Answers on Page 141*

Pronunciation

Exercise 8

PRONUNCIATION. Practice saying the following words.

1. Actress (*Ack*-triss)
2. During (*jer*-ring)
3. Foreign (*For*-rin)
4. Instrument (*In*-strih-mint)
5. Kilometer (*Kih*-*law*-mih-der)
6. Healthy (*Hell*-thee)
7. Helicopter (*Hel*-lih-cop-ter)
8. Marathon (*Mair*-ra-thawn)
9. Montreal (*Mon*-chree-all)
10. Religion (*Ree*-*lih*-gin)
11. Scuba dive (*Skoo*-ba-dive)
12. Soap opera (*Soap*-op-pra)
13. Whistle (*Wiss*-soe)
14. Wrap (*Rap*)

Exercise 9

TIME. **a.m. = morning** and **p.m. = afternoon and evening**. Now, Practice reading and saying the following.

1. 2:00 Two O'clock
2. 2:05 Two O-five
3. 2:08 Two O-eight
4. 2:10 p.m. Two ten p.m.
5. 2:15 Two fifteen
6. 2:25 Two twenty-five
7. 2:30 Two thirty
8. 2:40
9. 2:55 p.m.
10. 3:00
11. 3:05 a.m
12. 3:15
13. 3:30 a.m
14. 3:50
15. 4:00 p.m
16. 4:01 p.m
17. 4:05
18. 4:10
19. 4:14 a.m
20. 4:30
21. 4:40
22. 5:00
23. 5:05
24. 5:30

Exercise 10

CUMULATIVE REVIEW.

1. When is your birthday?
2. Is Hala Mountain in North Korea?
3. Do Japanese people speak Japanese?
4. Do you have a snowboard?
5. Do you think today is cold?
6. Does Pardeep play volleyball?
7. What are your hobbies?
8. What do you think of Kim Yu-na?
9. Which do you prefer, spring or summer?
10. Let's go shopping.

Unit 9: What Can You Do?

• **VOCABULARY:** Study the following words.

Beginner 초보자
Do you know how to...? ~하는 방법을 아세요?
During ~하는 동안
Far 먼
Foreign 외국의
Healthy 건강한
Helicopter 헬리콥터
Instrument 기구
Marathon 마라톤
Religion 종교
TV programs TV 프로그램
Whistle 휘파람 불다
Soap Opera
연속극

Dialogue

MORE VOCABULARY (VERBS):

Can…? ~할 수 있어요?
Clean 깨끗한
Climb 오르다
Drive 운전하다
Exercise 운동하다
Fix 고치다
Fly a kite 연을 날리다
Need 필요하다
Know how to ~하는 방법을 알다
Peel potatoes 감자를 벗기다

Rock climb 암벽등반하다
Scuba dive 스쿠버 다이빙 하다
Skydive 스카이 다이빙하다
Take photographs 사진 찍다
Tie your shoes 신발끈을 매다
Try 시도하다
Use chopsticks 젖가락을 사용하다
Whistle 휘파람 불다
Wrap a gift 선물을 포장하다

Exercise

DIALOGUE 1. With your class and then with your classmates, practice the following conversation. 다음 대화를 연습 하세요.

A: Sung-Min, are you busy right now?
    B: No, I'm not. Why?
A: Can you speak Japanese?
    B: Yes, I can speak Japanese. Why?
A: I need some help with my homework.
    B: Are you studying Japanese?
A: Yeah.
    B: Can't you speak Japanese?
A: No, I can't. I'm a beginner.
    B: Can your girlfriend speak Japanese?
A: No, she can't.
    B: Okay, I can help you.

Interview

Exercise 2

INTERVIEW 1: CAN? and CAN'T? "**Can you . . . ?**" = "**Can't you . . . ?**". Working in groups, practice the following questions. Can?과 Can't 구문을 연습 하세요.

1. Can you fly an airplane? *No, I can't fly an airplane.*
2. Can't you cook ramyon? *Yes, I can cook ramyon.*
3. Can't you make kimpap? *No, I can't make kimpap*
4. Can Boa sing well? *Yes, she can sing well.*
5. Can you swim?
6. Can you ski?
7. Can you drive?
8. Can you whistle?
9. Can we speak Korean?
Yes, we can speak Korean.
10. Can't you snowboard?
11. Can you speak English?
12. Can't you speak Chinese?
13. Can you fly a kite?
14. Can you fly a helicopter?
15. Can't monkeys climb trees?
16. Can children drink beer?
No, children can't drink beer.
17. Can't you take photos?
18. Can you walk 5 kilometers?
19. Can't you climb Halla Mountain?
20. Can Australians speak English?
21. Can Pardeep speak English?
22. Can your brother ride a bike?
23. Can't marathon runners run far?
24. Can Nicolas Cage act well?
25. Can Spiderman climb well?
26. Can Superman fly?
27. Which sports can you play? *I can play baseball, basketball and I can snowboard.*
28. Which instruments can you play? (*I can't play any instruments*) or (*I can play trhe piano and the guitar*)
29. Which languages can you speak?
30. What food can you cook?

Beer: by BovineMagnet

Dialogue

Exercise 3

DIALOGUE 2. ("Do you know how to. . . ?" = "Can you . . . ?")

A: Where do you live?
    B: I live in Montreal, in Canada.
A: How do you like Korea?
    B: I think Korea is wonderful.
A: Can you teach me some French?
    B: I'm sorry, I can't teach you French.
A: *Don't you* speak French?
    B: *No, I don't* speak French.
A: Isn't Montreal a French speaking city?
    B: Yes, it is. But I'm from Vancouver.
A: Vancouver*! Do you know how to* speak Chinese?
    B: Haha! *No, I don't know how to* speak Chinese.

Exercise 4

INTERVIEW 2: DO/DON'T YOU KNOW HOW? "Do you . . . ?" = "Don't you . . . ?" Again, practice your English conversation skills by asking your classmates the following questions.

1. Do you know how to drive? *Yes, I know how to drive.*
2. Do you know how to speak Spanish? *No, I don't know how to speak Spanish.*
3. Don't you know how to wrap a gift? *Yes, I know how to wrap a gift.*
4. Do you know how to fix computers? *No, I don't know how to fix computers.*
5. Don't you know how to make ice-cream? *No, I don't know how to make ice-cream.*
6. Do you know how to fix cars?
7. Don't you know how to drive?
8. Do you know how to skydive?
9. Do you know how to fly a kite?
10. Do you know how to scuba dive?
11. Do you know how to rock climb?
12. Do you know how to play Go-Stop?
13. Do you know how to peel potatoes?
14. Do you know how to speak Japanese?
15. Do you know how to do taek-won-do?
16. Don't you know how to cook spaghetti?
17. Don't you know how to play table tennis?

What Can She Do?

Exercise 5

WHAT CAN HE/SHE DO? Using the verbs from the list below, ask and answer each other questions: 먼저 아래의 동사들을 이용해 문장을 만들고 서로 묻고 답하세요.

cook   fly a kite   jog   play the guitar   ride a motorbike   skydive   vacuum
tie his shoe   take a photo   play basketball   use chopsticks

1. What can she do?
She can use chopsticks.

2. .... he do?
_____

3. .... do?
_____

4. ....?
_____

5. ....?
_____

6. ....?
_____

7. ....?
_____

8. ....?
_____

9. ....?
_____

10. ....?
_____

11. ....?
_____

Pronunciation

Exercise 6

PRONUNCIATION. With your class, practice pronouncing the following words:

1. Abroad (*a-brawd*)
2. Alcohol (***Al**-koe-hall*)
3. Always (***All**-weez*)
4. Early (***Er**-lee*)
5. Evening (***Eev**-ning*)
6. Frequency (***Free**-kwin-see*)
7. "Get a hair cut" (***Ghed**'a-hair-Kut*)
8. "Go to bed" (***Go**-dih-bed*)
9. Jog (*jawg*)
10. Mexico (***Meck**-sih-koe*)
11. Might (*Mite*)
12. Normally (***Nor**-moe-lee*)
13. Often (***Off**-tin*)
14. Once (*Wonce*)
15. Percent (*Per-**sent***)
16. Rarely (***Rair**-lee*)
17. Routine (***Roo**-teen*)
18. Station (***Stay**-shin*)
19. Travel (***Tra**-voe*)
20. Uniform (***U**-nih-form*)
21. Wake up (***Way**-cup*)

Haircut: by Mark Hillary

Crossword

CROSSWORD

Across
2. Can we _____ home and watch TV?
6. Can we _____ ?
11. Can't you _____ kimpap?
12. _____ you know how to snowboard?
13. I can play _____ piano.
14. Can you wrap a _____ ?
15. They're drinking _____
17. I have to _____ the floor.
19. Do you know how _____ do taek-won-do?
20. He can _____ his shoe.

Down
1. Let's _____ TV.
3. He can ride a _____
4. Can you use _____ ?
5. Can we _____ to the zoo?
6. Let's _____ a taxi.
7. Can't you _____ the guitar?
8. Can you _____ a marathon?
9. He's surfing the _____
10. I can't spend much _____
16. He will _____ his friends.
18. Can you _____ potatoes?

Answers on Page 141

Dates

Exercise 8

DATES. Practice saying the following. Look at page 45 for assistance.

1. August (*Aw-ghist*)
2. April (*A-pro*)
3. August 1 (*Aw-ghist first*)
4. August 2 (*Aw-ghist se-khind*)
5. August 3 (*Aw-ghist third*)
6. August 4 (*Aw-ghist fourth*)
7. August 9
8. April 14
9. April 22
10. May 19
11. June 23
12. July 3
13. January 6
14. December 25
15. November 11
16. March 1
17. September 30
18. December 31
19. January 1
20. April 3

Calendar: by Joe Lanman

Unit 10: Your Routine

- **VOCABULARY:** Again, study and practice saying the following words.

About 대략
Abroad 외국에
Alcohol 알코올
Always 항상
Almost 거의
Around 6:00 6시 정도
Early 일찍
Evening 저녁
Frequency 빈도
Haircut 이발
Just 단지, 막
Late 늦은
"Late at night" 저녁 늦게
Never 결코 ~ 하지 않다
Normally 보통은
Often 자주
Once 한번
"Once a week" 일주일에 한번
Percent (%) 퍼센트
Rarely 거의 ~ 하지 않다.
Routine 일상생활
Sometimes 때때로

Twice 두 번
"Twice a week" 일주일에 두 번
Uniforms 유니폼
Usually 보통
Weekends 주말
Weeknights 주중 저녁

Dialogue

MORE VOCABULARY (VERBS): Study and practice saying the following verbs and expressions.

Brush your teeth 양치질 하다
Chat 잡담 하다
Climb 오르다
Internet Chatting 인터넷 채팅
Do your banking 은행 일을 보다
Get a hair cut 머리깎다
Get home 집에 도착하다
Get off work 퇴근하다
Go to bed 잠자리에 들다
Jog 조깅하다
Relax 쉬다
Stay home 집에 있다
Travel 여행하다
Wake up 일어나다

Exercise 1

DIALOGUE. Practice the following conversation.

A: What do you *usually* do on Saturdays?
  B: On Saturdays, I *usually* go shopping, but *sometimes*, I stay home and relax.
A: How about on Sunday?
  B: On Sundays, I *always* go to church/stay home and watch TV/read. How about you?
A: I *usually* go to church/clean my house/go mountain climbing.
A: What do you do on weeknights?
  B: On weeknights, I often watch TV, but sometimes I just read.
A: When do you *usually* get home after work/school?
  B: I *usually* get home around 4:00/about 7:00/late at night.

Stained Glass: by DanieVDM

Words of Frequency

TIP 1: WORDS OF FREQUENCY. We can describe our routine and how often we do things by using the following "words of frequency". "빈도 부사"는 횟수를 나타냅니다.

Always	100 % of the time
Almost always	About 90-99% of the time
Usually = Normally	About 70-90%
Often = Frequently	About 40-80%
Sometimes = Occasionally	About 25-60%
Rarely = Hardly ever = Seldom	About 5-20%
Almost never	About 1-20%
Never	0%

Exercise 2

WORDS OF FREQUENCY. Fill in the blanks with the appropriate words from above. 위의 빈도부사를 이용해 빈칸을 채우세요.

1. I ... *almost never* .... play basketball.
2. I .... speak Korean.
3. My mother .... speaks Korean.
4. I .... eat kimchi.
5. I .... eat beef.
6. I .... eat dog (boshintang).
7. I .... watch TV.
8. Park Ji-jung .... plays well.
9. I .... vacuum the floor.
10. Children .... like candy.
11. Koreans .... eat kimchi.
12. I .... study English in the evening.
13. I .... drink soju on Friday evenings.
14. I .... go shopping on weekends.
15. I .... go to church on Sunday.
16. I .... wake-up early.
17. Brazilians .... play soccer.
18. Koreans .... play ice-hockey.
19. I .... go to Mexico.
20. I .... go to Gangnam Station.
21. I .... go to Japan
22. I .... go to Apu-jeong.
23. I .... go to Incheon.
24. I .... play golf.
25. Koreans .... watch TV dramas.
26. Children .... go to school on Monday.
27. Doctors .... wear white coats.
28. I .... take a shower in the morning.

Interview

Exercise 3

INTERVIEW 1: WHEN? Interview your classmates. Remember **normally** = **usually**.
친구들에게 인터뷰 하세요.

1. When do you usually *wake up*?
I usually wake up at 7:00 a.m.
I usually wake up around 7:00 a.m.
2. When do you normally take a shower?
I normally take a shower in the morning.
I normally take a shower at night.
3. When do you usually play soccer?
I usually play soccer on Sunday afternoon.
I normally play soccer on the weekend.
I never play soccer.
4. When do you normally study?
5. . . . . . usually go to sleep?
6. . . . . . eat breakfast?
7. . . . . . go shopping?
8. . . . . . brush your teeth?
9. . . . . . go to work/school?
10. . . . . get home after work/school?

Exercise 4

INTERVIEW 2: WHERE? Once again, interview your classmates.

1. Where do you usually meet your friends?
I usually meet my friends at the gym. (A)
I usually meet my friends at school. (A)
I usually meet them in Gangnam. (A)
I never meet my friends. (A)
I usually meet my friends at school, but sometimes I meet them at the gym. (A+)
I usually meet my friends at work, but sometimes I meet them at church. (A+)
2. Where do you usually study?
3. Where do you normally exercise?
4. Where do you usually eat lunch?
5. watch TV?
6. go shopping?
7. watch movies?
8. go snowboarding?
9. go for your vacation?
10. . . . . brush your teeth?
I usually brush my teeth in the . . . .

Interview

Exercise 5

INTERVIEW 3: WHAT? Once again, interview your classmates.

1. What do you normally eat for breakfast?
For breakfast, I normally eat rice. (A)
For breakfast, I normally eat kimchi and rice. (A+)
2. What do you normally do in the evening?
In the evening, I normally read. (A)
In the evening, I usually watch TV. (A).
In the evening, I usually read or study. (A+)
3. What do you normally eat for lunch?
4. What do you normally do in the evening?
5. What do you usually do during Chu-seok?
During Chu-seok, I usually go to my hometown.
During Chu-seok, I usually visit my grandmother's house.
6. What do you normally do on your birthday?
7. What do you usually eat when you're sick?
When I'm sick, I usually eat . . . . .
8. . . . . cook on the weekend?
9. . . . . do on Friday evenings?
10. . . . . drink when you're sick?
11. . . . . do on Saturday evenings?
12. . . . . do on Sunday mornings?
13. . . . . do on Sunday evenings?
14. . . . . do when you have a headache?
15. . . . . do when you meet your friends?
16. . . . . drink when you meet your friends?

Watching TV: by Giovanni Giusti

Specific Frequency

TIP 2: SPECIFIC FREQUENCY. We can specify exactly how often we do things by using some of the following expressions.

Never (I never . . . . .) 결코 ~하지 않다
Once a day 하루에 한번
Once a week 일주일에 한번
Once a month 한달에 한번
Once a year 일년에 한번
Twice a day 하루에 두번
About twice a day 하루에 두번 정도

Three times a week 일주일에 세번
Four times a month 한달에 네번
Five times a year 일년에 다섯번
About five or six times a year 일년에 다섯, 여섯번 정도
Every day 매일

Exercise

FILL IN THE BLANKS. Look at TIP 2 and then fill in the blanks with the appropriate answers.

1. I go to school . . . *every day* . . . .
2. I watch TV . . . .
3. I take a shower . . . .
4. I eat kimchi . . . .
5. I . . . . go to North Korea.
6. I study English . . . .
7. I go shopping . . . .
8. I . . . . climb Mount Everest.
9. I drink water . . . .
10. I meet my friends . . . .
11. I wake up early . . . .
12. I wash my hands . . . .

Mount Everest in Distance: by star_trooper

Interview

Exercise 7

INTERVIEW 4: HOW OFTEN? Again, interview your classmates.

1. How often do you jog?
I <u>never</u> jog.
I jog <u>every day</u>.
2. How often do you eat rice?
I eat rice <u>every day</u>.
I eat rice <u>three times a week</u>.
3. How often do you play soccer?
I play soccer <u>once a week</u>.
4. About how often do you swim?
I swim <u>about two or three times a year.</u>
5. How often do you eat kimchi?
6. How often do you drink water?
7. How often do you go to Taegu?
8. How often do you catch a cold?
9. How often do you get a hair cut?
10. How often do you go shopping?
11. How often do you play Go-Stop?
12. How often do you take a shower?
13. How often do you play StarCraft?
14. How often do you take the subway?
15. About how often do you drink alcohol?
16. About how often do we see each other?
17. About how often do you go to the bank?
18. How often do we have an English class?
19. How often do you go to a singing room?
20. How often does your sister play the piano?
21. How often do you speak to Lee Yeong-ae?

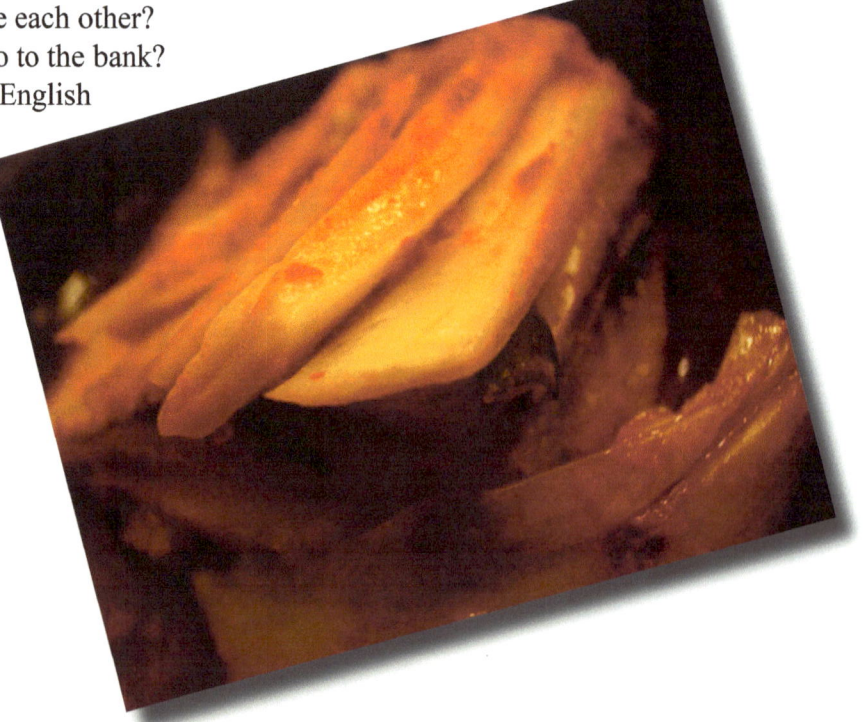

Kimchi by Live-gym Showtime

Pardeep's Schedule

Exercise 8

PARDEEP'S WEEKLY SCHEDULE. Again interview your classmates, asking questions about Pardeep's schedule. Pardeep의 스케줄에 대한 질문을 친구들에게 인터뷰 하세요.

PARDEEP'S WEEKLY SCHEDULE

	Sunday	Monday	Tuesday	Wednesday	Thursday	Friday	Saturday
Morning	Go to church	Go to school	Go to school	Go to school	Go to school	Go to school	Go to ABC English Academy
Morning	Play soccer						
Afternoon	Visit Grandmother				Swim		Play golf
Afternoon		Study	Study	Study	Study	Study	
Evening		Go jogging	Listen to music	Go jogging		Go jogging	
Evening	Watch movies	Study English	Watch TV	Study English	Read	Meet his friends	Go to movies

1. How often does Pardeep play soccer?
He plays soccer <u>once a week</u>.
2. How often does Pardeep go jogging?
3. How often does he study English?
4. How often does Pardeep meet his friends?
5. How often does he go to school?
6. How often does he go to church?
7. . . . . Pardeep swim?
8. . . . . he visit his grandmother?
9. . . . . he go to movies?
10. . . . . play soccer?
11. . . . . visit his uncle?
12. . . . . Pardeep play golf?

Exercise 9

CUMULATIVE REVIEW.

1. Who is your favorite actress?
2. Who is your favorite marathon runner?
3. Do you drink beer?
4. Can you sing *Yesterday*?
5. Do we have exams in this conversation class?
6. Do you walk to school?
7. What does Pardeep like to do in his free time?
8. What time do you usually get off work?
9. What are your hobbies?
10. When is your birthday?

11

Unit 11: Past Tense

• **VOCABULARY**: Study and practice saying the following words.

Already 이미
Anything else? 그 밖에 다른 일은요?
Afternoon 오후
Chicago Bulls 시카고 불스
Clean 깨끗한
Basketball 농구
Biography 일대기
Birth 탄생
Born 태어난
Cousin 사촌
During 동안
Excited 흥분한
Famous 유명한
Ghost 유령
Gifts 선물
Gold medal 금메달
Hungry 배고픈
Irregular verb 불규칙 동사
Last night 지난밤
Last week 지난주
Message 메시지
Pancakes 팬케익

Regular verb 규칙동사
Restaurant 식당
Sleepy 졸린
Take a break 쉬다
Team 팀
Vacation 휴가
Washington Wizards 워싱턴 위저드
What else? 다른 것은요?

Pronunciation

MORE VOCABULARY (VERBS): Study and practice saying the following verbs.

Attend 참석하다	Fight 싸우다	Open 열다
Clean 청소하다	Fly 날다	Park 주차하다
Begin 시작하다	Get married 결혼하다	Pay 지불하다
Break 깨다	Go to school 학교가다	Push 밀다
Bury 묻다	Have lunch 점심을 먹다	Practice 연습하다
Buy 사다	Hit 치다	Rain 비오다
Carry 나르다	Hold 붙들다	Send 보내다
Close 닫다	Hurry 서두르다	Start school 개학하다
Cry 울다	Improve 향상하다	Start work 일을 시작하다
Die 죽다	Laugh 웃다	Think 생각하다
Eat breakfast 아침 식사하다	Learn 배우다	Wake up 일어나다
Enjoy 즐기다	Look 보다	Want 원하다
Erase 지우다	Lose 잃다	Wash 씻다
Fail 실패하다	Love 사랑하다	Work 일하다
Fall down 넘어지다	Meet 만나다	
Feel 느끼다	Need 필요하다	

Exercise 1

PRONUNCIATION. Although many verbs have an "ed" ending, these endings have different sounds. With your class, practice saying the following words. 대부분의 동사 끝에는 "ed"가 붙는데 발음은 서로 다릅니다. 다음 단어를 말하면서 연습하세요.

1. Verbs ending with a **"d" sound**	2. Verbs ending with an **"id" sound**:	3. Verbs ending with a **"t" sound**.
Cleaned (*Cleend*)	Graduated (***Gra**-jew-ay-did*)	Cooked (*Cookt*)
Buried (***Bur**-read*)	Needed (***Nee**-did*)	Erased (***Ee**-raist*)
Closed (*Closd*)	Started (***Star**-did*)	Finished (***Finn**-nisht*)
Cried (*Cried*)	Snowboarded (***Snoe**-boar-did*)	Golfed (*gulft*)
Died (*Died*)	Visited (***Viz**-zi-did*)	Helped (*Helpt*)
Enjoyed (*In-**joid***)	Wanted (***Wan**-tid*)	Jumped (*Jumpt*)
Emailed (***E**-maild*)		Kissed (*Kist*)
Failed (*Faild*)		Laughed (*Laft*)
Hurried (***Hur**-read*)		Liked (*Likt*) ("eye" sound)
Learned (*Lernd*)		Looked (*Lookt*)
Listened (***Lih**-sind*)		Practiced (***Prack**-tist*)
Lived (*Livd*)		Walked (*Wahkt*)
Loved (*Lovd*)		Washed (*Washt*)
Married (***Mair**-read*)		Watched (*Wacht*)
Opened (***Oh**-pind*)		Worked (*Werkt*)
Played (*Playd*)		
Rained (*Raind*)		
Skied (*Skeed*)		
Studied (***Stuh**-deed*)		

103

Dialogue

Exercise 2

DIALOGUE.

A: Hi Ki-hoon. How are you?
  B: I'm fine.
A: How was your winter vacation?
  B: It was great! I *went* to New York City.
A: New York!
  B: Yes, I *visited* my uncle and his family.
A: What did you do there?
  B: I *worked* at my uncle's restaurant. I *cooked* and *cleaned* there.
A: What else did you do?
  B: I *attended* my cousin's wedding. She *got married*.
A: Did you do anything else?
  B: Sure. I *went* to the Empire State Building, *watched* some plays, *saw* an NBA basketball game, and I *practiced* my English.
A: Did your English improve?
  B: Yes, of course. It *improved* a lot. What did you do?
A: Nothing special. I *studied* TOEIC and *snowboarded* a few times.

GRAMMAR 1: SIMPLE PAST TENSE. To change regular verbs to the past tense, we add "**ed**" to the end of the verbs. 규칙동사의 과거형을 만들기 위해서 동사 끝에 "ed"를 붙인다.

For example:
Now,   I live   in Korea.
Last year, I liv**ed** in Japan.

For example:
This month, I play   soccer.
Last month,   I   play**ed** volleyball

Here are some more examples:

call - call**ed**
clean - clean**ed**

cook - cook**ed**
die - di**ed**
fail - fail**ed**
finish - finish**ed**
graduate from – graduat**ed** from
jump - jump**ed**
laugh - laugh**ed**
learn - learn**ed**
like - lik**ed**
listen to – listen**ed** to
live - liv**ed**
look - look**ed**
love - lov**ed**

need - need**ed**
open - open**ed**
play - play**ed**
ski - ski**ed**
start - start**ed**
talk – talk**ed**
visit – visit**ed**
walk - walk**ed**
want – want**ed**
wash - wash**ed**
watch – watch**ed**
work - work**ed**

Y Verbs

Exercise 3

FILL IN THE BLANKS. Fill in the blanks by changing the following to the past tense. 아래 동사를 과거형으로 바꾸고 빈칸을 채우세요.

fail   live   play   graduate   cook   walk   listen   watch

1. Last night, I . . . *watched* . . . . . . TV.
2. I'm tired because this afternoon, I . . . . soccer.
3. I . . . . my exam. I got an F.
4. My grandmother . . . . dinner. She's a great cook.
5. I think he's very smart. He . . . . from Yonsei University.
6. We . . . . to the radio.
7. We . . . . through the park. It was a nice walk.
8. Now, I live in Osan, but last year, I . . . . in Suwon.

GRAMMAR 2: "Y" VERBS. For the past tense, we change the "**y**" endings into "**ied**" endings. 과거형을 만들기 위해서 "**y**"로 끝나는 동사는 "**ied**"로 고친다.

Here are some examples:
bury - bur**ied**
carry – carr**ied**
cry – cr**ied**
hurry - hurr**ied**
marry - marr**ied**
study – stud**ied**

Soccer: by Ezalis

Irregular Verbs

GRAMMAR 3: IRREGULAR VERBS. For irregular verbs, we don't add "ed" to the end of the verb.
불규칙 동사는 동사끝에 "ed"를 붙이지 않는다.

For example:
Today, I eat rice
Yesterday, I ate potatoes

For example:
I have one exam
Last week, I had two exams

More examples:
be – was/were
begin - began
break - broke
buy – bought (*bawt*)
come - came
do - did
drink - drank

eat - ate
fall - fell
fall down – fell down
feel – felt
fight – fought (*fawt*)
fly – flew (*floo*)
get - got
get up – got up (*gaw-dup*)
get married – got married
go – went
have - had
hit - hit
hold - held
lose – lost (*lawst*)
make – made (*maid*)
meet - met

pay - paid
read – read (*red*)
ride - rode
run - ran
say – said (*sed*)
see - saw
send - sent
sleep – slept
speak - spoke
take - took
teach – taught (*tawt*)
think – thought (*thawt*)
wake-up – woke-up (***woe**-kup*)
win – won
write - wrote

Exercise 4

FILL IN THE BLANKS. Fill in the blanks with verbs from the following list, but change each verb to the past tense.

drink wake ride go send take buy get read write

1. My mother and father . . . *got* . . . married 25 years ago.
2. During my summer vacation, I . . . . to Europe.
3. Last week, I . . . . a new computer. It was 500,000 won.
4. Last night, my friends and I . . . . a lot of beer.
5. Yesterday, I . . . . the KTX.
6. During my vacation, I . . . . a lot of books.
7. John Grisham . . . . many famous novels.
8. On Sunday, I . . . . him three email messages.
9. This morning, I . . . . up at 7:30.
10. Last night, I . . . . a taxi home.

Past Tense

Exercise 5

PAST TENSE. Change the following verbs to the past tense. And then practice saying all the words. 다음 동사들을 과거형으로 바꾸고 연습 하세요.

1. be . . . *were/was* . . . . .
2. run . . . .
3. break . . . .
4. start . . . .
5. climb . . *climbed* . . .
6. carry . . . .
7. study . . . .
8. cook . . . .
9. do . . . .
10. drink . . . .
11. want . . . .
12. fall down . . . .
13. jump . . . .
14. teach . . . .
15. hold . . . .
16. get married . . . .
17. read . . . .
18. golf . . . .
19. have . . . .
20. hit . . . .
21. help . . . .
22. get . . . .
23. kiss . . . .
24. walk . . . .
25. talk . . . .
26. listen to . . . .

Rock Climbing: by Clinton Steeds

Past Tense

Exercise 6

PAST TENSE. Again, change the following verbs to the past tense and then practice saying them.

1. listen to. . . . .
2. live . . . .*lived*. . . . .
3. look at. . . . . . .
4. look for. . . . .
5. watch. . . . .
6. write. . . . .
7. play . . . .
8. practice. . . . .
9. push. . . . .
10. go . . . .
11. ride . . . .
12. begin. . . . .
13. send . . . .
14. skate. . . . .
15. skate board. . . . . .
16. speak . . . .
17. call. . . . .
18. clean. . . . .
19. visit . . . .
20. eat . . . .
21. learn. . . . .
22. wash. . . . .
23. lose. . . . .
24. win . . . .
25. make. . . . .
26. like . . . .
27. fly. . . . .

Skateboarding: by TXD

Interview

Exercise 7

INTERVIEW 1: DID/DIDN'T. In groups, ask each other the following questions:

1. Did you *work* yesterday?
<u>Yes</u>, I work<u>ed</u> yesterday.
<u>No</u>, I didn't work yesterday.
2. Did you *eat* rice yesterday?
<u>No</u>, I didn't eat rice yesterday
3. Did you *go* to school yesterday?
4. Did you *watch* TV last night?
5. Did you *go* shopping yesterday?
6. . . . .*go* to Japan last month?
7. . . . .*walk* to school today?
8. . . . .*speak* English yesterday?
9. . . . .*get married* yet?
<u>Yes</u>, I got married already.
<u>No</u>, I didn't get married yet.
10. . . . .*read* the newspaper yesterday?
11. . . . .*play* computer games last week?
12. . . . . *see Shrek*?
13. . . . .*kiss* anyone last week?
14. . . . .*listen to music* last week?

Newspaper Stands: by Will Hybrid

Interview

Exercise 8

MATCHING. Match the questions from Column A with the appropriate answers from Column B. 질문과 대답을 알맞게 연결 하세요.

COLUMN A:		COLUMN B:
1. What did you eat for breakfast?	I	A. I watched a movie.
2. What did you drink last night?	___	B. I drank beer.
3. Where did you go for your vacation?	___	C. I went to church.
4. Who did you meet yesterday?	___	D. I started at 9:00.
5. What time did you start work today?	___	E. I went to China.
6. What time did you finish work?	___	F. I had chicken.
7. What did you have for lunch?	___	G. I finished at 6:00.
8. What did you do on Sunday morning?	___	H. I met my friends.
9. What did you do last night?	___	I. I ate pancakes.
10. What did you see?	___	J. I saw a ghost.

Exercise 9

INTERVIEW 2: WHAT DID YOU DO? Once again, with your class and with your partner, ask and answer the following questions: 다시 한번 다음 문장들을 연습하세요.

1. What time did you go home yesterday? *Yesterday, I went home at 9:00.*
2. What did you eat last night? *Last night, I . . . . .*
3. What did you drink last night? *Last night, ...*
4. Where did you go yesterday?
5. What time did you go to bed last night?
6. When did you wake up today?
7. What did you eat for breakfast?
8. What time did you start work/school today?
9. Who did you meet yesterday?
10. What did you drink today?
11. Who did you see today?

110

Game

Exercise 10

INTERVIEW 3: YESTERDAY. Again, interview your classmates.

1. What did you do yesterday afternoon, at 2:00?
Yesterday at 2:00, I worked.
2. What did you do yesterday at 5:00 p.m.?
3. What did you do yesterday at 7:00 p.m.?
4. What did you do yesterday at 10:00?
5. What did you do this morning at 4:00?
6. What did you do today at 7:00?
7. What did you do today at 9:00?
8. What did you do on your birthday?

Exercise 11

GAME. In this game, one person, "the speaker", will read out any of the following three lists of verbs. Read one word at a time, in the same order that they appear in the list. Another person(s) will respond by stating the past tense form of the same word. This person cannot look at the book. If he or she has a teammate, these teammates must take turns answering or responding. However, each teammate can only speak when it's his or her turn.

For example, the speaker will begin the game by reading out the first verb from the list and then another person (one person only) answers by shouting out the past tense form of the same verb. If he or she gets the right answer, it counts as one point. If the answer is incorrect, no points are awarded. His or her teammate will then try to answer the next (the second) verb. For the third verb, the first teammate will shout the answer and so on. If a person gives a wrong answer, the speaker should then quickly move on to the next verb. If a player does not know the answer, he or she can say "pass" instead of wasting time. When this happens, he loses his turn and the speaker moves on to the next verb (and if there's a teammate, the next teammate). Each correct answer is one point. Someone (this can be the speaker) must keep track of the points. After one minute, the speaker stops reading out the verbs. This can be a one-to-one competition or a competition between teams (2-5 teammates are okay). Before playing the game, the teacher should give the students five or ten minutes to prepare and study. Students should play the game several times to improve their English. LEVEL 3 is the most difficult level.

Game Starts on Next Page

Game

LEVEL 1
1. eat - ate
2. go - went
3. do - did
4. be – was/were
5. have - had
6. get - got
7. go - went
8. see - saw
9. come - came
10. play - played
11. run - ran
12. marry - married
13. drink - drank
14. get - got
15. like - liked
16. visit - visited
17. cook - cooked
18. study - studied
19. win - won
20. eat - ate
21. take - took
22. start - started
23. pay - paid
24. cry - cried
25. talk - talked
26. make - made
27. snowboard (…ed)
28. open - opened
29. read - read
30. enjoy - enjoyed
31. fall - fell
32. hit - hit
33. eat - ate
34. lose - lost
35. send - sent
36. win - won
37. teach - taught
38. wash - washed
39. marry - married
40. walk - walked
41. call - called
42. hold - held
43. like - liked
44. start - started

LEVEL 2
1. go - went
2. teach - taught
3. do - did
4. be - was
5. have - had
6. get - got
7. buy - bought
8. see - saw
9. help - helped
10. play - played
11. run - ran
12. hurry - hurried
13. practice - practiced
14. get - got
15. email - emailed
16. fail - failed
17. say - said
18. carry - carried
19. win - won
20. teach - taught
21. erase - erased
22. buy - bought
23. love - loved
24. cry - cried
25. graduate from – graduated from
26. make - made
27. ski - skied
28. want - wanted
29. read - read
30. rain - rained
31. fall - fell
32. hit - hit
33. eat - ate
34. lose - lost
35. send - sent
36. win - won
37. teach – taught
38. fly - flew
39. fight - fought
40. hurry - hurried
41. lose - lost
42. break - broke
43. practice - practiced
44. take - took

LEVEL 3
1. fight - fought
2. go - went
3. do - did
4. be – was/were
5. have – had
6. get - got
7. buy - bought
8. see - saw
9. speak - spoke
10. wake-up – woke-up
11. fight - fought
12. bury - buried
13. break - broke
14. get - got
15. begin - began
16. fail - failed
17. say - said
18. carry - carried
19. win - won
20. fight - fought
21. feel - felt
22. buy - bought
23. sleep – slept
24. cry - cried
25. fly - flew
26. make - made
27. get married – got married
28. get up – got up
29. read - read
30. think - thought
31. fall - fell
32. hit - hit
33. eat - ate
34. lose - lost
35. send - sent
36. win - won
37. run - ran
38. ride - rode
39. begin - began
40. speak - spoke
41. meet - met
42. drink - drank
43. fall - fell
44. read - read

Pronunciation

Exercise 12

PRONUNICATION.

1. Agree (*a-gree*) 동의하다
2. Bull (*Boe*)
3. Carolina (*Kair-roe-line-ah*)
4. Chicago (Shih-**kah**-go) 시카고
5. Christmas (*Kriss-miss*) 크리스마스
6. Elementary (*El-lih-men-tree*) 초등의
7. Excited (*ick-sigh-did*) 흥미진진한
8. Hospital (*Haws-bih-doe*) 병원
9. Party (*Par-D*) 파티
10. Scary (*Scair-ree*) 무서운
11. Tired (*Tie-urd*) 피곤한
12. Washington (*Wash'ing-tin*) 워싱턴
13. Wizards (*Wiz'urds*) 위저드

Exercise 13

CUMULATIVE REVIEW.

1. Are you Buddhist?
2. Let's take a break!
3. Do you have an iPod?
4. Do you live in Wonju?
5. What does Pardeep like to do?
6. Do you know how to play golf?
7. Did you surf the Internet yesterday?
8. How many computers do you have?
9. Where do you usually go shopping?
10. How often do you wash your hands?

Buddhists: by Devadath

12

Unit 12: Past Tense (Part 2)

- **VOCABULARY**: Study and practice saying the following words.

Angry 화난
Chicago Bulls 시카고 불스
Christmas Day 성탄절
Elementary School 초등학교
"Four years ago" 4년전
Gold medal 금메달
Hospital 병원
Hungry 배고픈
"Interested in" 관심이 있는
Meeting 모임
North Carolina 북 케롤라이나
Party 파티
Retired 은퇴한
Rainy 비오는
Scary 무서운
Summer Olympics 하계 올림픽
Team 팀
Terrified 무서워하는
Tired 피곤한
Until 까지
Washington Wizards
워싱턴 위저드

Was/Were

MORE VOCABULARY (VERBS): Study and practice saying the following verbs.

Brush your teeth 양치질 하다
Do yoga 요가 하다
Comb your hair 머리 빗다
Finish 끝내다
Get dressed 옷을 입다
Graduate from 졸업하다
Play for 경기를 하다

Retire 은퇴하다
Swam 수영했다
Talk on the telephone 전화 통화하다
Take a shower 샤워하다
Tie your shoe 신발끈을 매다
Went to church 교회에 갔다

GRAMMAR 1: WAS/WERE. For the past tense, "is" changes to "**was**" or "**were**". Study the examples below, and then try the following exercise. "is"의 과거형은 "**was**" 또는 "**were**" 이다. 예문을 공부하고 연습문제를 풀어 보세요.

Today	Yesterday
I am	I was
You are	You were
He is	He was
She is	She was
It is	It was
We are	We were
They are	They were

EXAMPLES:
1. **Today**, I **am** happy, but **yesterday**, I **was** sad.
2. Yesterday, **you were** tired.
3. Last week, **he was** in the hospital.
4. Four years ago, **she was** in high school.
5. Today it is sunny, but yesterday, **it was** rainy.
6. **We were** excited about the party.
7. In 2003, **they were** students.

Exercise 1

FILL IN THE BLANKS. Use "**was**", or "**were**", 빈칸에 "was," 또는 "were를 넣으세요.

1. When I ..*was*... in elementary school, I lived in Incheon.
2. During the 2002 FIFA World Cup, he . . . . only eight years old.
3. She . . . . my piano teacher when I . . . . in elementary school.
4. We . . . . terrified because the movie . . . . very scary.
5. I didn't go to work yesterday because I . . . . sick.
6. My sister didn't watch the movie. She . . . . too sleepy.
7. They . . . . very angry because I ate all of the ice cream.
8. We . . . . at the night club until 5:00 a.m.!
9. Michael Jordan . . . . born in 1963, in New York City.
10. Koreans . . . . very angry when Ono won the gold medal.

Wasn't/Weren't

GRAMMAR 2: WASN'T/WEREN'T. For the past tense, the expressions "am not,", "is not," and, "are not" become either "**was not**" or "**were not**". Study the examples below, and then try to do the following exercise. "am not", "is not,"과 "are not"의 과거형은 "**was not**" 또는 "**were not**" 이다.

Today
I am not   I'm not
You are not   You aren't
He is not   He isn't
She is not   She isn't
It is not   It isn't
We are not   We aren't
They are not   They aren't

Yesterday
I was not   I wasn't
You were not   You weren't
He was not   He wasn't
She was not   She wasn't
It was not   It wasn't
We were not   They weren't
They were not   They weren't

EXAMPLES:
1. **Today**, **I'm** happy, but **yesterday**, I **wasn't** happy.
2. Yesterday, **you weren't** tired.
3. Last week, **he wasn't** at work.
4. Four years ago, **she wasn't** working.
5. Yesterday, **it wasn't** rainy.
6. **We weren't** excited about the party.
7. In 2003, **they weren't** old enough.

Exercise

FILL IN THE BLANKS. Fill in the blanks with "**was**," "**wasn't**", or "**weren't**" 빈칸에 "**was**," "**wasn't**", 또는 "**weren't**" 중 알맞은 표현을 넣으세요.

1. My mother . . . . not born in Seoul.
2. They . . . . at the meeting.
3. I . . . . happy. I was sad.
4. Michael Jordan . . . . born in 1963.
5. We . . . . hungry because we had no food.
6. She . . . . born in the 1980's. She was born in the 1970's.
7. It . . . . very cold and snowy.
8. Yesterday . . . . sunny. It was rainy.
9. You . . . . interested in music? Why not?
10. No, I . . . . not.
11. He . . . . not at home.
12. John Lennon . . . . an actor.

Interview

Exercise 3

INTERVIEW 1: WAS/WASN'T. Once again, with your partner, ask and answer the following questions. Use, "*was*" and "*wasn't*" in your answers.
다음 문장들을 "*was*" 또는 "*wasn't*"를 넣어 대답하면서 연습 하세요.

1. Were you in China last year?
Yes, I was in China last year.
No, I wasn't in China last year.
2. Were you in the hospital last year?
3. Were you sick yesterday?
4. Was your father in Pusan yesterday?
No, my father wasn't in Pusan yesterday.
5. Were you born in the 1980's?
6. Were you born in the 1990's?
7. Were you born in Seoul?
8. Was your mother born in Seoul?
9. Were you in Korea last year?
10. Were you happy last night?
11. Were you studying yesterday?
12. Were you drinking last night?
13. Was it hot yesterday?
14. Was yesterday Friday?
No, yesterday wasn't Friday.
Yes, yesterday was Friday.
15. Was yesterday Tuesday?
16. Was yesterday cold?
17. Was Won Bin in the movie, *Taeguki*?
18. . . . . *Chingu* a good movie?
19. . . . . *Shrek* a sad movie?
20. . . . . . yesterday a rainy day?

Haeundae Beach, Pusan: by Frakorea

What Did You Do?

Exercise 4

INTERVIEW 2: WHAT DID YOU DO? Ask and answer the following questions. Try to state at least **five** things that you did. 다음 문장들을 연습하면서 여러분이 했던 일을 최소한 다섯 개 이상 말하세요.

1. What did you do on Sunday morning?
<u>On Sunday morning</u>, I went to church. (B)
<u>On Sunday morning</u>, I woke up, ate breakfast <u>and then</u> went to church. (A-)
<u>On Sunday morning</u>, I woke up, took a shower, got dressed, ate breakfast <u>and then</u> went to church. (A+)
2. What did you do on your birthday?
<u>On my birthday</u>, I went to work, went home, met my friends, went to Pizza Hut, <u>and</u> opened my birthday gifts. (A+)

3. What did you do on Christmas day?

4. What did you do last year?

5. What did you do last week?

6. What did you do on Sunday?

7. What did you do last night?

8. What did you do today?

Christmas Bulb: by Krisdecurtis

118

Schedule

Exercise 5

WHAT DID PARDEEP DO? Ask your classmates about what Pardeep did last week.
Pardeep이 지난주에 했던 일들에 대해 서로 질문 하세요.

PARDEEP'S SCHEDULE FOR LAST WEEK

	Sunday	Monday	Tuesday	Wednesday	Thursday	Friday	Saturday
Morning.	Go to church	Go to school	Go to school	Go to school	Go to school	Go to school	Go to ABC English Academy
Morning		Play soccer					
Afternoon	Visit Grandmother				Swim		Play golf
Afternoon.		Study	Study	Study	Study	Study	
Evening		Go jogging	Listen to music	Go jogging		Go jogging	
Evening	Watch movies	Study English	Watch TV	Study English	Read	Meet his friends	Go to movies

1. What did Pardeep do on Sunday evening?
On Sunday evening, Pardeep watched movies.
2. What did he do on Monday?
On Monday, he went to school, studied, went jogging *and then* studied English.
3. What did Pardeep do on Tuesday morning?
4. What did Pardeep do on Tuesday afternoon?
5. . . . . on Tuesday evening?
6. . . . . on Wednesday evening?
7. What did he do on Thursday?
8. . . . . on Friday?
9. . . . . on Saturday afternoon?
10. . . . . . . on Sunday morning?

Michael Jordan

Exercise 6

MICHAEL JORDAN. Ask each other questions about Michael Jordan. Michael Jordan에 대해 다음을 질문 하세요.

Michael Jordan

February 17, 1963: Born in New York City
1960's: Lived in New York City.
1970: Moved to North Carolina.
1970's: Lived in North Carolina.

1970's: Played baseball, football and basketball.
1978-1981: High School
1981-1984: University of North Carolina.
1981-1984: University of North Carolina Basketball team.

1984: Summer Olympics: Team USA → Gold medal.

1984-1993: NBA: Chicago Bulls basketball team

1986: Finished University

1992: Summer Olympics: Team USA: Gold medal

1993: No basketball. Played baseball
1994-1998: NBA: The Chicago Bulls basketball team
1998-2000: Retired. No basketball
2001 – 2003: NBA: Washington Wizards basketball

1. When *was* Michael Jordan *born*?
He was born in 1963.
2. Where *was* Michael *born*?
3. When did Michael *move to* North Carolina?
4. When did Michael *start* University?
5. When did Michael *win* a gold medal?
6. When did Michael *graduate from* University?
7. When did Michael *play* baseball?
8. Where did Michael *live* in 1965?
In 1965, Michael lived in . . . . .
9. Where did Michael *live* in 1968?
10. Where did Michael *live* in 1972?
11. Which sports did Michael play in the 1970's?
In the 1970's, Michael played . . . ., ..., and . . . .
12. Which University did Michael *go to*?
13. What did Michael *win* in 1984?
14. Which team did Michael *play for* in 1986?
In 1986, Michael played for the . . . .
15. Which team did Michael *play for* in 1991?
16. *Did* Michael play basketball in 1999?
17. *Did* Michael play basketball in 2001?
18. Which team did Michael *play for* in 2002?
19. Was Michael in the 1984 Summer Olympics?
Yes, he was in the 1984 Summer Olympics.
20. Was Michael born in 1985?
21. Was Michael born in New York City?
22. Was Michael a baseball player in 1993?
23. Was Michael a Chicago Bull in 1996?

120

Game

Exercise 7

GAME. Working alone, or with your team (each team member taking turns to speak), state what each of the following people DID. The fastest team is the winner. Each team or participant should be able to accomplish this exercise in under a minute. Each mistake is a two second penalty!

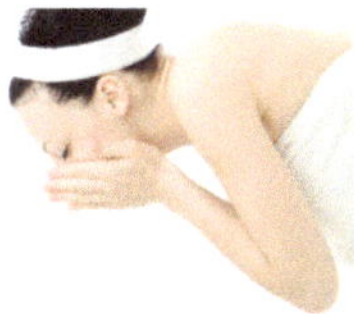

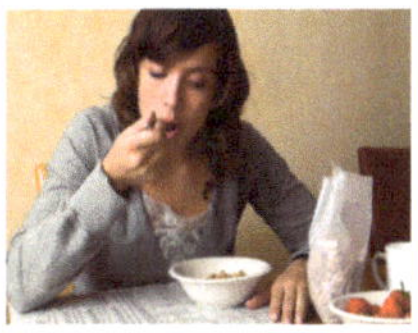

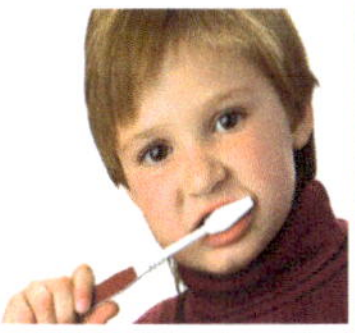

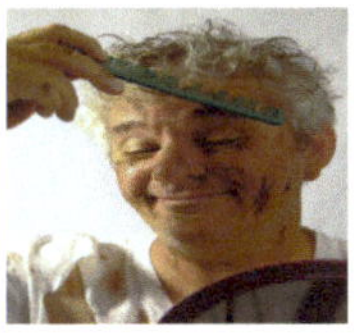

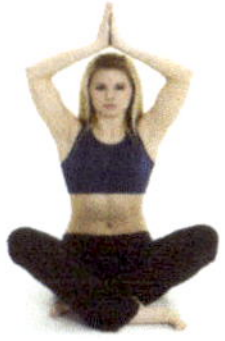

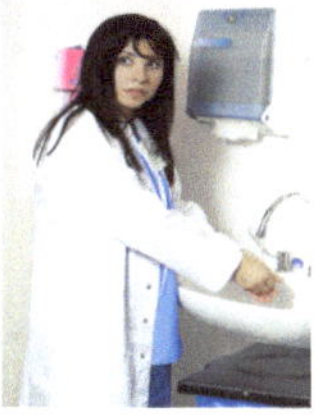

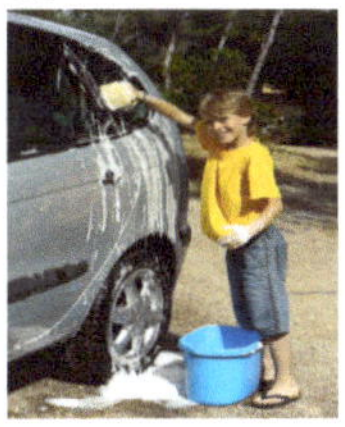

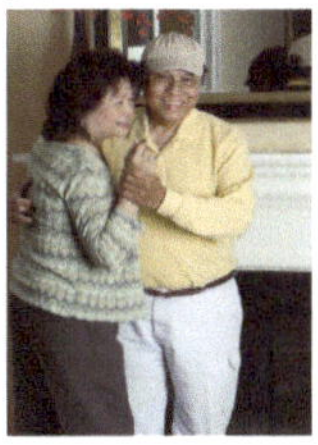

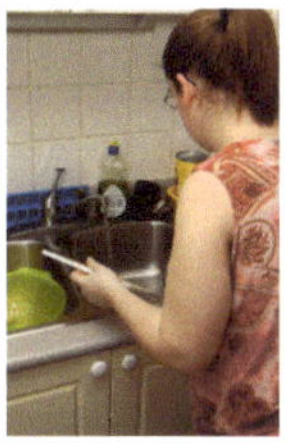

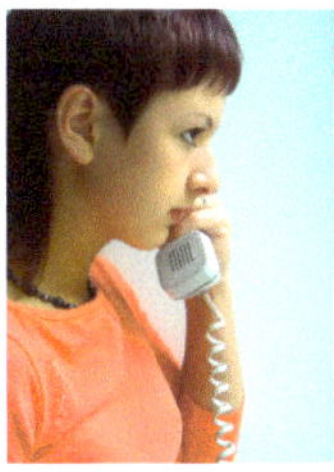

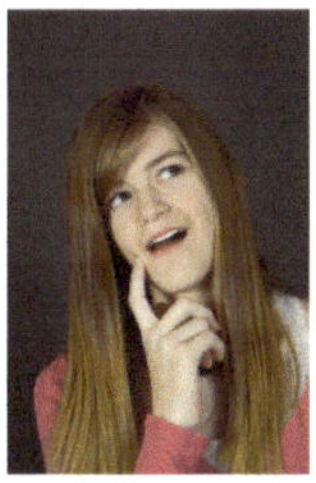

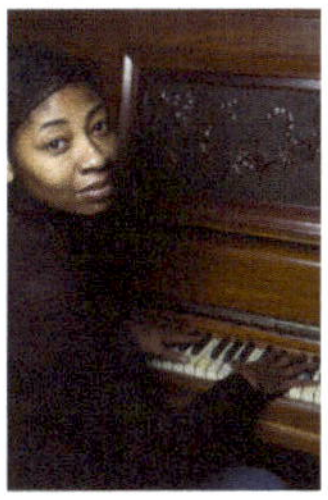

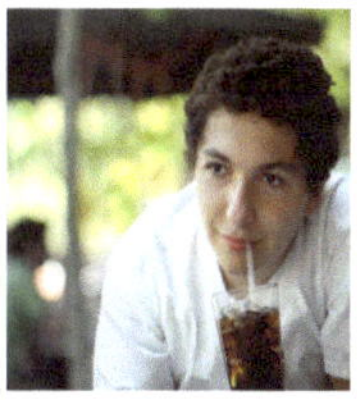

1. He woke up
2. She washed her face
3. She ate breakfast
4. He brushed his teeth
5. He combed his hair
6. She did yoga
7. She washed her hands
8. He washed the car
9. They danced
10. She washed/did the dishes
11. She talked/spoke on the phone
12. She thought
13. She played the piano
14. She went rock climbing
15. He flew a kite
16. He watched TV
17. They swam
18. He cooked
19. They studied
20. They went whitewater rafting
21. She tied her shoe
22. They fought
23. She drank milk
24. He took a photo/took photos
25. He drank Coke/Cola

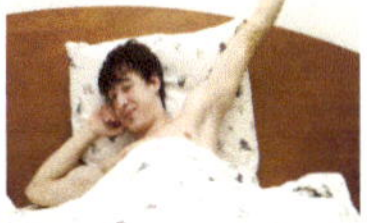

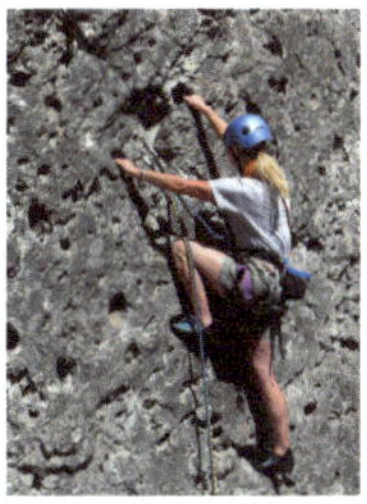

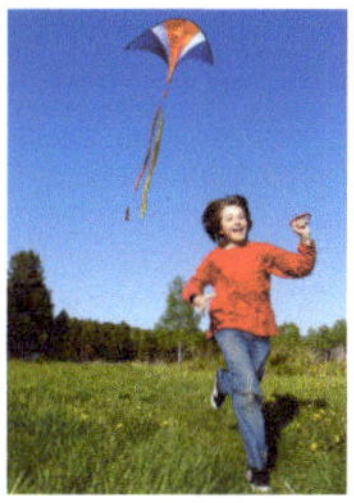

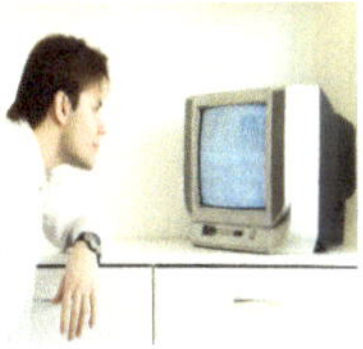

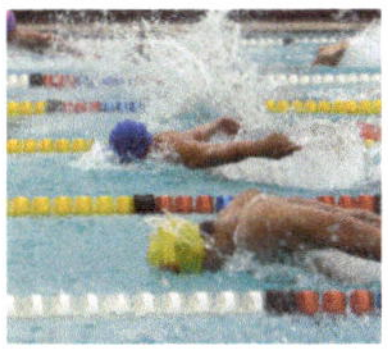

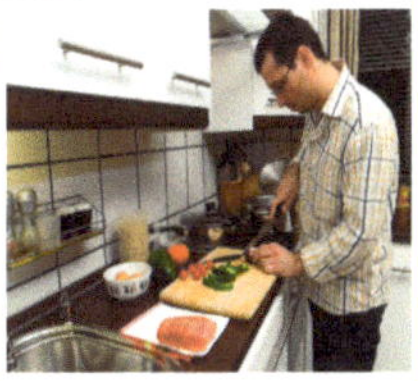

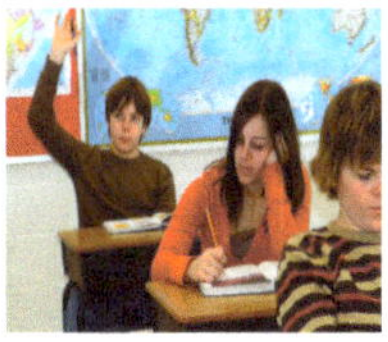

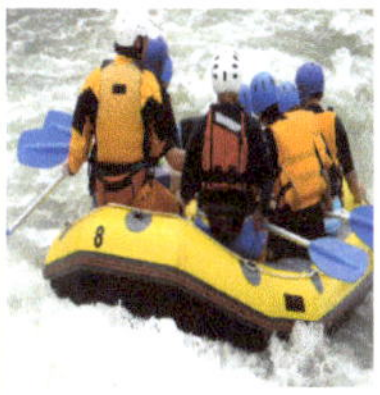

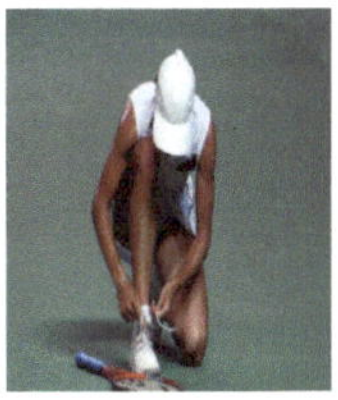

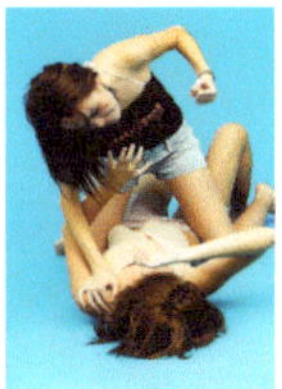

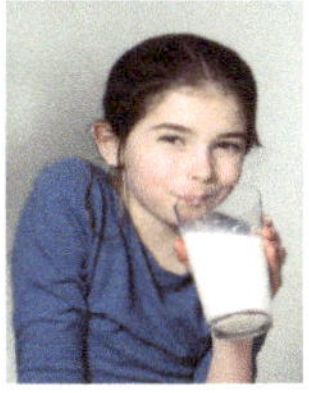

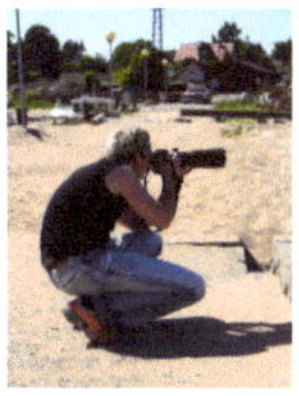

Pronunciation

Exercise 8 PRONUNCIATION.

1. Autumn (*Aw-dim*)
2. Cloud (*clowd*)
3. Definitely (*Def'in'it-ley*)
4. Get a hair cut (*Ghed'a haircut*)
5. Massage (*Mah-sawj*)
6. Probably (*Praw-bah-blee*)
7. Sleep-in (*Slee-pin*)
8. Thai (*Tie*)
9. Warm (*Worm*)
10. "You'd better…" (*Yood bedder*)

Exercise 9 CUMULATIVE REVIEW.

1. Where does your family live?
2. Is Guam in South Korea?
3. Does Pardeep go jogging?
4. Do you have hiking boots?
5. How often do you drink milk?
6. Can Americans speak English?
7. Did you do yoga yesterday?
8. Did you talk on the phone yesterday?

Unit 13: Future and Weather

VOCABULARY: Study and practice saying the following words.

Cloud 구름
Cold 추운
Cool 시원한
Definitely 분명히
"Definitely won't"
Download 다운로드하다
Evening 저녁
Fall (Autumn) 가을
Fast Food Restaurant 패스트 푸드 음식점
"Five years from now."
Freezing 몹시추운
Haircut 이발
Hot 더운
Light 밝은
Massage 마사지
Maybe 아마도
Might ~ 일 것이다
Perfect 완벽한
Picnic 소풍
Probably 아마도
"Probably won't"
Rain 비

Rainy 비오는
Snow 눈
Snowy 눈오는
Spring 봄
Summer 여름
Sun 해
Terrible 형편없는
Thai 타이
Thai massage 타이 마사지
Umbrella 우산
Warm 따뜻한
Wind 바람
Windy 바람부는
Winter 겨울
Wonderful 훌륭한

Dialogue

MORE VOCABULARY (VERBS): Study and practice saying the following verbs.

Attend a meeting 모임에 착석하다
Download 다운로드 받다
Forecast 예상하다
Get a hair cut 이발하다
I think 나는 ~ 라고 생각한다
Rain 비가 오다

Sleep-in 늦잠자다
Snow 눈오다
Why don't you join us? 우리랑 같이 하실래요?
You'd better… 당신은 ~ 하는게 낫다
You should… 당신은 ~ 해야만 한다

DIALOGUE.

A: What'll you do tomorrow night?
    B: I think I'll stay home.
A: Stay home!
    B: Yeah. I think I'll just relax and watch TV. How about you?
A: I'll meet my friends: Hyun-Jin, Jung-eun, and Seung-min.
    B: Where?
A: We'll probably meet downtown somewhere and then go to VIPS.
    B: VIPS! I love VIPS.
A: Why don't you join us?
    B: Okay, that sounds great! I will.

HOW'S THE WEATHER? For each of the following, ask each other "**How's the weather?**" or "**What's the weather like?**"

1. "How's the weather?"
It's warm
2. "What's the weather like?"
It's hot
3. _____ It's cool
4. _____ It's windy
5. _____ It's rainy
6. _____ It's snowy
7. _____ It's sunny
8. _____ It's cloudy

9. _____ It's nice
10. _____ It's beautiful!
11. _____ It's wonderful!
12. _____ It's perfect!
13. _____ It's terrible!
14. _____ It's raining
15. _____ It's snowing
16. _____ It's freezing

How's The Weather?

Exercise 3

HOW'S THE WEATHER. Look at the following photos and ask your classmates "**How's the weather?**" or "**What's the weather like?**"

1. . . . . ? It's	2. . . . . ? It's . . . .
3. . . . . ? It's	4. . . . . ? It's . . . .
5. . . . . ? It's	6. . . . . ? It's . . . .
7. . . . . ? It's	8. . . . . ? It's . . . .

Will You...?

MATCHING. First, match the words in Column A with the appropriate words and phrases in Column B. Then, practice saying the expressions.

COLUMN A		COLUMN B
1. It's freezing!	_____	A. You'd better wear a warm winter coat!
2. It's so cool!	_____	B. Let's go snowboarding.
3. It's rainy.	_____	C. Let's go to the beach.
4. It's perfect.	__D__	D. Let's go for a picnic.
5. It's very sunny.	_____	E. You should wear a sweater.
6. It's hot.	_____	F. Let's fly a kite.
7. It's windy.	_____	G. You'd better take an umbrella.
8. It's snowy.	_____	H. Don't forget your sunglasses!

WILL YOU...? With your class and then working in groups, ask and answer the following questions. Be sure to use *will* or *won't* in your answers. 다음 문장들을 *will* 또는 *won't* 넣어 대답하면서 연습 하세요.

1. Will you go to New York this month?
<u>No, I won't go to New York this month.</u>
2. Will you eat kimpap next month?
<u>Yes, I will eat kimpap next month.</u>
<u>Yes, I'll eat kimpap next month.</u>
3. Will you stay home tonight?
<u>Yes, I will stay home tonight.</u>
<u>Yes, I'll stay home tonight.</u>
<u>No, I won't stay home tonight.</u>
4. Will you watch TV tonight?
5. Will you sleep-in on Sunday?
6. Will you eat lunch tomorrow?
7. Will you visit Japan this year?
8. Will you study English tonight?

9. Will you eat pizza next month?
10. Will you get a haircut tomorrow?
11. Will you go to work tomorrow?
12. Will you get married next year?
13. Will you go to school tomorrow?
14. Will you go to church on Sunday?
15. Will you go to Jejudo on Saturday?
16. Will you study English next week?
17. Will you go shopping on Saturday?
18. Will you have an English class next week?
19. Will you watch a movie on Saturday?
20. Will you drink beer on Friday evening?
21. Will you listen to an MP3 player today?
22. Will you play soccer on Sunday afternoon?

Will

GRAMMAR 1: FUTURE TENSE. We can talk about the future by adding "**will**" before a verb. For example, "*I will eat.*" To sound more fluent, you can say "*I'll eat.*" (**I will = I'll**) Study and practice saying the following: 동사뒤에 "will"을 넣어 미래형을 나타내는데, "*I will eat.*"는 "*I'll eat.*"로 줄일 수 있다. 다음 줄임말을 연습 하세요.

EXAMPLE 1:

I		I'll
You		You'll
He		He'll
She	will =	She'll
It		It'll
We		We'll
They		They'll

EXAMPLE 2:

I		eat lunch
You		drink
He		study
She	will	play
It		watch TV
We		exercise
They		swim

EXAMPLE 3:

Today, *he live**s*** in Osan.	**Next Year**, *he **will** live* in Osan.	Next year, ***he'll** live* in Osan.
Now, *she work**s***.	**Tomorrow**, *she **will** work*.	Tomorrow, ***she'll** work*.
This week *is* cool.	**Next week *will* be** cool.	

EXAMPLE 4: "WILL BE" and "WON'T BE"

I am – I **will** be	I**'ll** be	I am not - I **won't** be
You are – You **will** be	You**'ll** be	You are not – You **won't** be
He is – He **will** be	He**'ll** be	He is not – He **won't** be
She is – She **will** be	She**'ll** be	She is not – She **won't** be
It is – It **will** be	It**'ll** be	It is not – It **won't** be
We are – We **will** be	We**'ll** be	We are not – We **won't** be
They are – They **will** be	They**'ll** be	They are not – They **won't** be

EXAMPLE 5: "WILL GO" and "WON'T GO"

I **will** go	I**'ll** go	I **won't** go
You **will** go	You**'ll** go	You **won't** go
He **will** go	He**'ll** go	He **won't** go
She **will** go	She**'ll** go	She **won't** go
It **will** go	It**'ll** go	It **won't** go
We **will** go	We**'ll** go	We **won't** go
They **will** go	They**'ll** go	They **won't** go

Will

Exercise 6

MULTIPLE CHOICE. Choose the best answers.

1. What will you do tomorrow?
    a. I will go to Seoul
    b. I go to Seoul
    c. I play StarCraft

2. How's the weather?
    a. It's rain
    b. It's rainy
    c. It rainy

3. Will you go to Dongdaemun?
    a. No, I go to the Dongdaemun.
    b. Yes, I won't go to Dongdaemun.
    c. No, I won't go to Dongdaemun.

4. Will you sleep-in?
    a. Yes, I'll sleep-in
    b. Yes, can sleep-in.
    c. Yes, I sleep-in.

5. When will you leave?
    a. I'll leave at 6:00
    b. I leave at 6:00
    c. I leaving now

6. How will you get there?
    a. I'll get there by bus
    b. I'll get by bus
    c. I go by bus

7. Will it be sunny tomorrow?
    a. Yes, it will warm
    b. No, it's cool and wet.
    c. Yes, it will be sunny tomorrow.

8 Will it be warm tomorrow?
    a. Yes, tomorrow warm
    b. Yes, it's warm
    c. Yes, it'll be warm.

Exercise 7

WILL. For each of the following, write one proper sentence by including the word "**will**." Use the future tense.

1. Tomorrow, I pizza
Tomorrow I'll eat pizza.
Tomorrow, I will eat pizza.

2. Next week, I go Seoul.
_____

3. Tonight, you TV.
_____

4. Tomorrow, he music.
_____

5. Next year, go she Danguk University.
_____

6. Tonight, we English.
_____

7. Tonight, he vacuum the floor.
_____

8. Friday night, I StarCraft
_____

Probability

TIP: PROBABILITY. Often you don't know what will happen in the future. In these cases, you can use **might, maybe, possibly, probably** and **definitely**.
미래에 확실하지 않은 어떤 일을 표현할 때는 might, maybe, possibly, probably, definitely를 이용한다.

PROBABILITY

Maybe (>0%)	Maybe won't (<100%)
Possibly (>0%)	Possibly won't (<100 %)
Might (>0%)	Might not (<100%)
Probably (>50 %)	Probably won't (<50%)
Definitely (100 %)	Definitely won't (0%)

EXAMPLES

Maybe, I will go there.	**Maybe**, I **won't** go there.
Maybe, he'll speak English.	**Maybe**, He **won't** speak English.
Possibly, she will go jogging.	**Possibly**, she **won't** go jogging.
Possibly, they'll play golf.	**Possibly**, they **won't** play golf.
I **might** take a shower.	I **might not** take a shower.
He **might** use chopsticks.	He **might not** use chopsticks.
You will **probably** get married.	You **probably won't** get married.
It'll **probably** rain.	It **probably won't** rain.
I will **definitely** do my homework.	I **definitely won't** do my homework.
We'll **definitely** download the file.	We **definitely won't** download the file.

Exercise 8

TRUE OR FALSE. State whether the following statements are true (T) or false (F).

1. Tomorrow, I'll probably meet my friends. _____
2. Tonight, I will definitely surf the Internet. _____
3. Tomorrow, I will definitely laugh. _____
4. Next week, I might not take a shower. _____
5. Tomorrow, it might snow. _____
6. Tomorrow, it definitely won't snow. _____
7. Maybe, next month, I'll get married. _____
8. Next month, I will probably drive a taxi. _____
9. Tomorrow, I probably won't peel potatoes. _____
10. Today, my English might improve. _____
11. Next week, I won't go to school. _____
12. Tonight, I will probably write a letter. _____
13. Tomorrow, I'll definitely eat rice. _____
14. Next week, I might get a haircut. _____

Interview

Exercise 9

INTERVIEW 1: WHAT WILL . . . ? Ask and answer the following questions with your partner(s). You can use **maybe, possibly, might, probably** and **definitely**.

1. What will you do tomorrow?
Tomorrow, I'll attend a meeting.
Tomorrow, I might go downtown.
Maybe, tomorrow, I will stay home.
Tomorrow, I'll probably stay home and watch TV
2. What will you do tonight?
3. Where will you go tonight?
4. What will you eat tonight?
5. When will you eat tonight?
6. What will you eat tomorrow morning?
7. Where will you eat tomorrow morning?
8. What will you do tomorrow morning?
9. Where will you go tomorrow morning?
10. What will you do tomorrow evening?
11. What will you do on Saturday morning?
On Saturday morning, I'll probably go to the library.
12. Where will you go on Saturday evening?
13. What will you do on Sunday morning?
14. Where will you go Sunday afternoon?
15. Where will you go on your next vacation?
On my next vacation, I might go to the sea.
16. What will you do on your birthday?
17. What will you do next year?
18. Where will your family live next year?
19. When will you get married?
I don't' know when I'll get married.
20. When will you eat dinner?
21. Where will you live, five years from now?
In five years from now, I'll live in Mok-dong.
22. Where will you live, ten years from now?

Morning: by Elsie Esq.

Pronunciation

Exercise 10 — PRONUNCIATION.

1. April 14 (*A-pro four-teenth*)
2. Cabaret (*Ka'ba-ray*)
3. Phuket (*Poo-ket*)
4. August 7 (*Aw-ghist se-vinth*)
5. August 18 (*Aw-ghist A-teenth*)
6. Climb (*Clime*)
7. Iron (*I-rin*)
8. Laugh (*Laff*)
9. Scuba (*Skoo-ba*)
10. Shave (*Shaiv*)
11. Tour (*Toor*)

Exercise 11 — CUMULATIVE REVIEW.

1. What's your email address?
2. Do you feel sick?
3. Which do you prefer, Coke or Pepsi?
4. Does Seoul have a subway?
5. What is your favorite fast food restaurant?
6. Do you know how to play the guitar?
7. What do you usually do on your birthday?
8. How often do you use chopsticks?
9. How often does Pardeep play golf?
10. Did you get a haircut last week?
11. Was yesterday your birthday?
12. Was Michael Jordan born in 1960?

Seoul Subway: by Nakedsky

14

Unit 14: Future and Weather (Part 2)

• **VOCABULARY**: Study and practice saying the following words.

Barbeque 바베큐
Cabaret show 카바렛 쇼
Evening 저녁
Forecast 예보
Humid 습한
Iron 철
Ladder 사다리
Laundry 빨래
Phuket 푸켓 섬
Push-ups 팔굽혀 펴기
Rugby 럭비
Thai massage 타이 마사지
Volleyball 배구
Weather Forecast 일기예보

Dialogue

MORE VOCABULARY (VERBS): Study and practice saying the following verbs.

Arrive 도착하다
Attend a meeting 모임에 참석하다
Barbeque 바비큐하다
Board a plane 비행기 타다
Check-in to a hotel 호텔에 체크인하다
Check-out of the hotel 호텔에 체크아웃하다
Climb a ladder 사다리에 오르다
Do the laundry 빨래하다
Do push-ups 팔굽혀 펴다
Download 다운로드하다
Finish 끝내다

Forecast 일기예보하다
Hug 포옹하다
Iron clothes 철옷
Laugh 웃다
Need 필요하다
Shave 면도하다
Sweep 청소하다
Trek 가벼운 등산하다
Walk the dog 개를 산보시키다
Wash your face 세수하다

Exercise 1

DIALOGUE AT A KOREAN HOTEL. Practice this conversation.

A. May I help you?
    B. Yes, we'd like to go to Everland.
A. Everland? That's a good idea!
    B. *Will* it be open every day this week?
A. Yes, it *will*. When would you like to go?
    B. What's the weather forecast for this week?
A. Tomorrow *will* be cool.
    B. *Will* it rain?
A. No, it *'ll* be cool and sunny.
    B. How about Wednesday?
A. You can go on Wednesday, but you *'ll* need an umbrella.
    B. Okay. *We'll* go there tomorrow.

Everland: by iloveconor

Mun-hee's Vacation

Exercise 2

MUN-HEE'S THAI VACATION. Ask each other questions about Mun-hee's Thai vacation. 미나의 타이 여행에 대해 서로 질문 하세요.

MUN-HEE'S THAI VACATION

	Sunday	Monday	Tuesday	Wednesday	Thursday
7:00 a.m.			Wake-up		Wake-up
9:00 a.m.	Wake-up	Wake-up	Eat breakfast	Wake-up and eat	Eat
10:00 a.m. Morning	Go to Incheon Airport	Eat breakfast and read the newspaper	Go scuba diving	Go on a boat tour	Maybe go elephant trekking
12:00 p.m. Afternoon	Arrive at Incheon Airport	Go to the beach	Scuba diving		
1:00 p.m. Afternoon			Scuba diving		
2:00 p.m. Afternoon	Board her plane		Scuba diving	Go to the beach	Check-out of her hotel
4:00 p.m. Afternoon		Walk around town	Return to the hotel		Go to the Airport
6:00 p.m. Evening	Arrive at Phuket Airport	Go shopping on the street	Go to a Thai restaurant	Get a Thai Massage	
8:00 p.m. Evening	Check-in to her hotel	Eat at a Thai restaurant	Go to a cabaret show	Eat at a Thai Restaurant	
10:00 p.m. Evening	Go to sleep	Go to a bar	Probably go to a night club	Walk around town	
12:00 a.m. Evening		Maybe go to bed		Probably go to bed	Arrive at Incheon Airport.
2:00 a.m. Evening			Go to bed		

1. Where will Mun-hee go on Sunday?
<u>On Sunday</u>, she'll go to Phuket.
2. What will Mun-hee do on Monday morning?
<u>On Monday morning</u>, she will wake-up, eat breakfast <u>and</u> read the newspaper.
3. What will Mun-hee do on Monday evening?
<u>On Monday evening</u>, she will go shopping on the street, eat at a Thai Restaurant, go to a bar, <u>and then</u> maybe go to bed.
4. What will Mun-hee do on Tuesday morning?
5. . . . . Mun-hee do on Tuesday evening?
6. . . . . Mun-hee do on Wednesday evening?
7. . . . . do on Thursday morning?
8. When will Mun-hee arrive at the Phuket airport?
<u>She'll arrive at the Phuket airport on Sunday</u>, <u>at</u> 6:00 p.m.
9. When Will Mun-hee get a Thai massage?
10. . . . . . Mun-hee go scuba diving?
11. . . . . . Mun-hee check-out of her hotel?
12. . . . . eat at a Thai restaurant?
<u>She'll eat at a Thai restaurant on Monday, Tuesday and Wednesday evening.</u>
13. . . . . go to the beach?
14. . . . . go shopping?
15. . . . . go to a Cabaret show?
16. What will Mun-hee do on Sunday at 2:00?
<u>On Sunday at 2:00, she'll board her plane.</u>
17. What will Mun-hee do on Sunday at 8:00 p.m.?
18. . . . . . Mun-hee do on Tuesday at 9:00 a.m.?
19. . . . . do on Tuesday at 10:00 p.m.?
20. . . . . do on Thursday, at 10:00 a.m.?

Forecasts

Exercise 3

FORECASTS. Now practice saying the following forecasts:

1. It'll rain
2. It'll be rainy
3. It'll be cloudy and rainy
4. It'll snow
5. It'll be windy
6. It'll be warm and sunny
7. It'll be hot
8. It'll be hot and dry
9. It'll be hot and humid
10. It'll be cold

Exercise 4

WILL IT BE…? Look at the illustrations below and then ask and answer the following questions.

1. Will it be sunny tomorrow?
No, it won't be sunny tomorrow.
2. Will it be rainy on Wednesday?
3. Will it be windy on Thursday?
4. Will it be sunny on April 14?
No, it won't be sunny on April fourteenth.
5. Will it be snowy on January 17?
6. Will it rain on November 22?
7. Will it be cold August 7?
8. Will it be cold on January 20?
9. Will it be cool on July 26?
10. Will it be hot on August 18?
11. Will it be sunny on June 20?
12. Will it be nice on June 12?

1. Tomorrow	2. Wednesday	3. Thursday

4. April 14	5. January 17	6. November 22

7. August 7	8. January 20	9. July 26

10. August 18	11. June 20	12. June 12.

Weather Forecast

Exercise 5

WEATHER FORECAST. Look at the illustrations on the previous page and ask each other questions about the weather forecast. 위의 그림을 보면서 일기예보에 대해 서로 질문 하세요.

1. How will the weather be tomorrow?
Tomorrow will be rainy and windy.
It will be rainy and windy.
2. How will the weather be on Wednesday?
3. How will the weather be on Thursday?
4. . . . . . the weather be on April 14?
On April fourteenth, it will be very cloudy.
5. . . . . weather be on January 17?
6. . . . . be on . . . . . ?
7. What's the weather forecast for August 7?
On August seventh, it will be hot.
8. What's the weather forecast for January 20?
9. . . . . . forecast for July 26?
10. . . . . . forecast for . . . . . ?
11. . . . . for . . . . . ?
12. . . . . for . . . . . ?

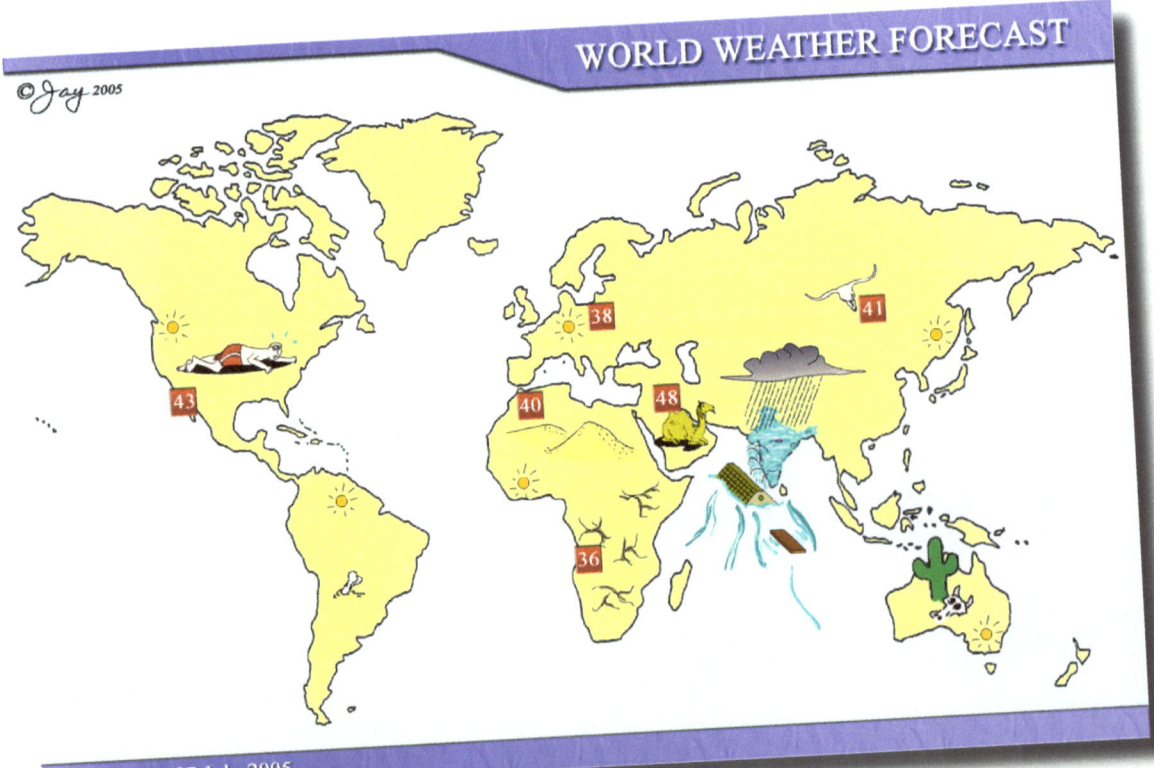

World Weather Forecast: by Jay Khemani

Game

Exercise 6

GAME. Working alone, or with your team (each team member taking turns to speak), state what WILL happen. The fastest team is the winner. Each team or participant should be able to do all of these in under a minute. Each mistake is a two second penalty!

START → 1 ... 35 Finish

1. He will wake up
2. He will wash his face
3. He will brush his teeth
4. He will shave
5. They will get married
6. He will watch TV
7. He will play basketball
8. They will do the laundry/wash clothes
9. He will walk the dog
10. She will talk on the phone
11. He will snowboard
12. He will smoke
13. They will play rugby
14. He will read the newspaper
15. It will rain
16. She will play volleyball
17. He will listen to music
18. He will laugh
19. They will hug
20. He will eat lunch/eat a sandwich
21. She will drink beer
22. She will do yoga
23. She will do the laundry/wash clothes
24. He will do push-ups
25. He will cry
26. He will cook
27. He will barbeque
28. He will climb a ladder
29. He will brush his teeth
30. They will drink beer
31. He will sweep
32. He will take a photo/picture
33. She will iron clothes
34. She will go shopping
35. They will finish

Review

CUMULATIVE REVIEW.

1. What is your telephone number?
2. Is Gus Hidink a good coach?
3. How many clocks do you have?
4. Do you like watching American movies?
5. Can you make kimpap?
6. What do you usually do on New Year's day?
7. How often do you surf the Internet?
8. How often does Pardeep go to school?
9. What did you do yesterday?
10. Where did Michael Jordan live in 1966?

Addendum: Verb-Noun Collocations

1. Arrive at the airport
2. Attend a meeting
3. Believe in God
4. Board a plane
5. Brush your teeth
6. Buy a computer
7. Check-in to a hotel
8. Check-out of the hotel
9. Clean the apartment
10. Climb a ladder
11. Climb a mountain
12. Climb a tree
13. Collect stamps
14. Comb your hair
15. Cook breakfast
16. Cook dinner
17. Cook food
18. Cook spaghetti
19. Dig a hole
20. Do homework
21. Do housework
22. Do push-ups
23. Do the dishes
24. Do the laundry
25. Do taek-won-do
26. Do yoga
27. Do your banking
28. Download a file
29. Drink beer
30. Drink Coke
31. Drink Cola
32. Drink green tea
33. Drink milk
34. Drink Pepsi
35. Drink soju
36. Drive a car
37. Drive a taxi
38. Drive a truck
39. Eat a meal
40. Eat fish
41. Eat ice cream
42. Eat kimchi
43. Fail an exam
44. Feel sick
45. Fix cars
46. Fly a helicopter
47. Fly a kite
48. Fly an airplane
49. Forget your sunglasses
50. Get a haircut
51. Get dressed
52. Get married
53. Get off work
54. Go outside
55. Go scuba diving
56. Go to a movie
57. Go to a sauna
58. Go to a soccer game
59. Go to the beach
60. Go to the library
61. Go to Caribbean Bay
62. Go to church
63. Go rock climbing
64. Go whitewater rafting
65. Go to school
66. Go to Daegu
67. Go to university
68. Go to work
69. Go to the bank
70. Graduate from university
71. Hate George Bush
72. Have an English class
73. Have coffee
74. Have lunch
75. Help sick people
76. Iron clothes
77. Lift weights
78. Listen to an MP3 player.
79. Listen to music
80. Listen to the radio
81. Live in Mok-dong
82. Live in Suwon
83. Make kimpap
84. Make noise
85. Meet your friend
86. Move to North Carolina
87. Peel potatoes
88. Play baseball
89. Play basketball
90. Play cards
91. Play chess
92. Play computer games
93. Play for the Chicago Bulls
94. Play for the Washington Wizards
95. Play golf
96. Play Go-Stop
97. Play hockey
98. Play Monopoly

Verb-Noun Collocations

99.	Play rugby	145.	Vacuum the carpet
100.	Play soccer	146.	Vacuum the floor
101.	Play sports	147.	Visit grandmother
102.	Play StarCraft	148.	Wake-up early
103.	Play tennis	149.	Walk a kilometer
104.	Play the guitar	150.	Walk the dog
105.	Play the piano	151.	Walk through the Park
106.	Play volleyball	152.	Walk to school
107.	Practice English	153.	Wash clothes
108.	Prefer Coke	154.	Wash the car
109.	Prefer Pepsi	155.	Wash the dishes
110.	Read a book	156.	Wash your face
111.	Read a novel	157.	Wash your hands
112.	Read comics	158.	Watch a DVD
113.	Ride a bicycle	159.	Watch baseball
114.	Ride the KTX	160.	Watch hockey
115.	Run a marathon	161.	Watch TV
116.	See a basketball game	162.	Watch a movie
117.	See a ghost	163.	Watch a play
118.	Sell hotdogs	164.	Wear a coat
119.	Send email	165.	Wear a sweater
120.	Sing a song	166.	Wear boots
121.	Smoke cigarettes	167.	Win the gold medal
122.	Speak Chinese	168.	Work at a restaurant
123.	Speak English	169.	Work for Samsung
124.	Speak Korean	170.	Wrap a gift
125.	Speak Spanish	171.	Write a letter
126.	Speak on the phone	172.	Write an exam
127.	Spend money		
128.	Start school		
129.	Start university		
130.	Start work		
131.	Stay home		
132.	Study English		
133.	Study history		
134.	Study Japanese		
135.	Surf the Internet		
136.	Sweep the floor		
137.	Take a bath		
138.	Take a shower		
139.	Take a taxi		
140.	Take an umbrella		
141.	Take care of children		
142.	Take the subway		
143.	Tie your shoes		
144.	Use chopsticks		

Addendum: Answers

Page 84 (Crossword Puzzle):
Across:
1. play
2. sounds
5. do
6. meet
9. bike
15. swimming
17. should
18. any
19. run
21. are
22. home

Down
2. listen
3. sure
4. shopping
7. room
8. lets
10. why
11. dinner
12. movie
13. idea
14. have
16. we
20. too

Page 92 (Crossword Puzzle):

Across:
2. stay
6. takephotographs
11. make
12. do
13. the
14. gift
15. beer
17. sweep
19. t0
20. tie

Down
1. watch
3. bike
4. chopsticks
5. go
6. take
7. play
8. run
9. internet
10. money
16. meet
18. peel

Index

A

Accent 38, 46, 63

B

Be 7, 22, 127, 135

C

Can 88, 90
Conversation 83
Countries 64
Crossword 84, 92

D

Dates 93
Dialogue 14, 15, 20, 30, 41, 49, 55, 66, 71, 74, 79, 87, 89, 95, 104, 124, 133
Did 109, 110, 118, 119, 121
Do 31, 32, 33, 38, 57, 59, 71, 72, 89, 90, 110, 118, 119
Does 31, 32, 38, 67
Doesn't 33, 36, 56
Don't 17, 33, 55, 56, 89

E

Eat 36
Expressions 18, 78

F

Forecasts 135
Frequency 96, 99

G

Game 47, 111, 121, 137
Grammar 22, 31, 32, 34, 55, 60, 67, 104, 105, 106, 115, 116, 127

H

Have 55, 56, 57, 59
Hobbies 68, 70
How Many 60, 61

Index

How Much 71

I

Interview 16, 21, 23, 24, 26, 34, 36, 37, 42, 52, 57, 59, 62, 68, 69, 73, 74, 88, 89

J

Jordan 120

L

Let's 80
Like 69, 71

N

Nationalities 75
Numbers 17, 18, 27, 63

O

Order 45

P

Past 104, 107, 108
Play 34, 35
Present 34, 35, 50
Probability 129
Pronunciation 17, 27, 28, 39, 53, 63, 75, 76, 85, 91, 103, 122, 131

Q

Questions 15, 25, 42, 45, 78

R

Review 39, 46, 50, 53, 64, 76, 85, 101, 113, 122, 131, 138
Rewriting 17, 75

S

Silent Syllables 39

T

Time 85

Index

Tip 17, 27, 38, 39, 63, 96, 99

V

Vocabulary 13, 19, 29, 30, 40, 41, 49, 54, 65, 66, 77, 78, 86, 87, 94, 95, 102, 103, 114, 115, 123, 124, 132, 133

W

Wasn't 116, 117
What 72, 73, 74, 90, 98, 110, 118, 119, 130
When 97
Where 97
Writing 42, 45

www.ingramcontent.com/pod-product-compliance
Lightning Source LLC
Chambersburg PA
CBHW041525220426
43670CB00002B/29